# URBAN HOUSING
# FINANCE

ORGANISATION FOR ECONOMIC CO-OPERATION AND DEVELOPMENT

Pursuant to article 1 of the Convention signed in Paris on 14th December, 1960, and which came into force on 30th September, 1961, the Organisation for Economic Co-operation and Development (OECD) shall promote policies designed:

- to achieve the highest sustainable economic growth and employment and a rising standard of living in Member countries, while maintaining financial stability, and thus to contribute to the development of the world economy;
- to contribute to sound economic expansion in Member as well as non-member countries in the process of economic development; and
- to contribute to the expansion of world trade on a multilateral, non-discriminatory basis in accordance with international obligations.

The original Member countries of the OECD are Austria, Belgium, Canada, Denmark, France, the Federal Republic of Germany, Greece, Iceland, Ireland, Italy, Luxembourg, the Netherlands, Norway, Portugal, Spain, Sweden, Switzerland, Turkey, the United Kingdom and the United States. The following countries acceded subsequently through accession at the dates hereafter: Japan (28th April, 1964), Finland (28th January, 1969), Australia (7th June, 1971) and New Zealand (29th May, 1973).

The Socialist Federal Republic of Yugoslavia takes part in some of the work of the OECD (agreement of 28th October, 1961).

Publié en français sous le titre:

LE FINANCEMENT DU LOGEMENT
EN MILIEU URBAIN

The historical development of housing finance and tax systems in OECD countries has led to a pattern of subsidies which obscures the real cost of housing. As a result, many countries have experienced difficulty in achieving the basic objectives of equity and efficiency in their housing policies. In addition, housing policies have had important effects upon the location and condition of the urban housing stock and on the distribution of socio-economic groups within cities which have sometimes worked against the harmonious economic, environmental and social development of cities.

This report is the result of a three-year study undertaken within the framework of the OECD Urban Affairs Programme. It is based upon reports provided by OECD governments concerning the overall direction of their housing policies and main concerns; on two in-depth studies on "Tax Policies and Urban Housing Markets" and "The Maintenance and Modernisation of Urban Housing"; and on the results of a Seminar on Housing Investment and Urban Change.

The report advises governments to determine more clearly the appropriate role of central and local government in housing. It argues that more cohesive and consistent housing strategies should be developed which take more account of the inter-relationships between the different types of tenure arrangements available on urban housing markets. The report also examines the role housing policies can play in supporting or initiating urban regeneration. Finally, it recommends that governments should aim at developing pricing and rent structures which reflect more fully the real cost of housing and the value of housing services provided.

The report was written by Mr. Ray Robinson in cooperation with the OECD Secretariat. Mr. Robinson is Reader in Economics at the University of Sussex and policy analyst at the King's Fund Institute London.

Mr. Gavin Wood of Murdoch University, Perth, Australia and Prof. Duncan MacLennan, Director of the Housing Research Group of the University of Glasgow, United Kingdom, also acted as consultants and provided substantial input to the report via the in-depth studies on "Tax Policies and Urban Housing Markets" and on "The Maintenance and Modernisation of Urban Housing". The Synthesis of National Reports referred to in the report was written by OECD consultant, Mr. Bruce Chapman.

3

*Also available*

## MANAGING AND FINANCING URBAN SERVICES (May 1987)
(97 87 04 1) ISBN 92-64-12951-0   94 pages    £6.00    US$11.00    F60.00    DM22.00

## REVITALISING URBAN ECONOMIES (September 1987)
(97 87 06 1) ISBN 92-64-12979-0   102 pages    £6.00    US$13.00    F60.00    DM26.00

## URBAN POLICIES IN JAPAN (October 1986)
(97 86 05 1) ISBN 92-64-12886-7   108 pages    £8.00    US$16.00    F80.00    DM35.00

## MANAGING URBAN CHANGE:
Volume I: Policies and Finance (May 1983)
(97 83 02 1) ISBN 92-64-12442-X   136 pages    £8.50    US$17.00    F85.00    DM38.00

Volume II: The Role of Government (November 1983)
(97 83 04 1) ISBN 92-64-12478-0   114 pages    £5.00    US$10.00    F50.00    DM25.00

# TABLE OF CONTENTS

# INTRODUCTION

The economic, social and environmental problems of urban areas have become the focus of attention in practically all OECD countries in recent years. Ageing infrastructure, industrial restructuring and relocation, labour market dislocation, declining levels of public service provision and deterioration of the housing stock are developments which are common to many countries and which have serious implications for the quality of life and the welfare of people living in cities. Moreover, the international economic recession of the late 70s and 80s, which intensified the impact of these long run trends, also resulted in a tightening of the constraints on public expenditures and restricted the scope of national and local governments in their efforts to deal with these problems.

In some countries, the above concerns have an added dimension. Expanding urban populations continue to encounter housing shortages and a lack of infrastructure investment. This situation is similar to that faced by the more developed OECD countries during the 50s and 60s, but the economic climate of the 80s makes the task of coping with it particularly formidable.

During the first stage (1980-83) of the OECD's Urban Programme, housing policies frequently came to the forefront of countries' concerns, especially in relation to the supportive role which investment to maintain, modernise and rehabilitate housing can play in strategies to regenerate urban areas.

At the April 1983 meeting of the Group on Urban Affairs at Ministerial Level, Ministers stressed the need to develop more effective measures to provide, improve, maintain and renew urban housing. They noted in particular that national programmes for housing and urban renewal represented an important proportion of direct public expenditure in urban areas and should, therefore, be assessed for their effects in order to permit greater selectivity and targeting.

A project to review urban housing finance policies in Member countries was therefore identified as one of the three main priority areas for work by the Group on Urban Affairs under its 1983-86 programme.

## Policy Context

Urban housing finance policies in OECD Member countries reflect national and local housing objectives as well as broader social and economic concerns. The balance between these objectives, supported by a multiplicity of policy instruments, varies from country to country and changes over time.

Governments in OECD countries, therefore, pursue policies which either directly or indirectly are intended to influence the demand for and supply of housing. In most countries, housing credit accounts for more than one third of total credit in the economy and expenditure on housing ranges between 10 and 20 per cent of an average household's budget. The implications of improving the efficiency of public expenditure on housing and of generally achieving more satisfactory operation of housing finance systems are clearly important for national economies.

In the post-war period, public sector investments in housing provision increased markedly in response to serious housing shortages, leading in many countries to the development of large estates of public housing on the periphery of cities and, subsequently, to programmes of urban renewal in inner city areas. These patterns of investment have strongly affected urban spatial and economic structures and hence shape the context in which many current housing policy concerns have emerged.

By the 70s, in most OECD countries, the crude shortage of housing units had been largely removed. Investment in social rented housing was reduced, while economic growth, housing subsidies, rising incomes and inflation provided a context in which the construction of housing for owner occupation flourished.

In recent years, in many OECD countries, although overall demand for new housing construction has fallen, reduced levels of new housing construction are still required to cater for inter- and intra-regional population movements, the replacement of obsolete stock and the development of new life-styles. The broad balance of household numbers and housing units has also created an important shift of emphasis towards the maintenance, modernisation and rehabilitation of the existing housing stock.

In the Mediterranean countries of the OECD overall housing supply and housing quality problems remain serious. Rural-urban migration continues and illegal construction of housing, which is often sub-standard, and a lack of accompanying infrastructure are key issues. The experience of the more developed OECD countries in meeting post-war housing shortages can provide insights into the policies which these countries might develop in the 80s and 90s to provide adequate housing for their urban populations.

In most OECD countries, however, concerns about the overall supply of housing have now been either supplemented or replaced by questions concerning housing prices, affordability, social segregation, maintenance and modernisation, and neighbourhood quality. For these reasons, governments are still substantially involved in housing finance, directly through subsidies and government loan guarantees and, indirectly, through tax concessions and regulations. In addition new policy concerns are emerging as a consequence of the re-appraisal of the balance between public and private provision, changing responsibilities between central and local governments and the introduction of new techniques of housing management. These changes have all created a new context for the operation of housing policies in urban areas.

Government policy towards housing has also been affected recently by a combination of macro-economic factors, including lower economic growth, the diverse impacts of structural change on cities, inflation and volatile interest rates. Major effects of these macro-economic trends have been, first, to compound economic adjustment problems in certain cities, contributing to a deterioration of the supply and quality of the urban housing stock which, in turn, has erected barriers to the effective regeneration of these urban economies. Also, these trends have put considerable strain on housing finance systems and have frequently limited the amount of finance available for the production of new housing, both publicly and privately supplied, as well as reducing the finance available for maintaining and improving the existing stock.

In summary, there has generally been a shift in focus of policy interest away from problems of housing shortage towards maintenance and improvement, accompanied by increasing reliance on and encouragement of the private provision of housing. Finally, macro-economic factors have placed a strain on urban economies, on housing finance systems and public expenditure directed at the housing sector.

In view of these trends governments have been giving increasing attention to:

a) Reassessing housing finance policies with a view to improving their efficiency and equity, in the present climate of scarce resources;

b) Introducing policies to encourage a more satisfactory operation of urban housing markets, in particular, increasing adaptability to inflation and volatile interest rates; and

c) Promoting the role of housing finance policies as an instrument of urban regeneration.

In the light of these circumstances, the OECD Group on Urban Affairs decided to examine how housing finance policies in Member countries are affecting cities with a view to assisting the process of reframing housing policy objectives in urban areas and to identifying innovative approaches to achieving them under new conditions.

OECD Project on Urban Housing Finance

The specific objectives of this project are:

a) To identify the interrelationships between economic, social and environmental trends and changes in the urban housing finance policies of Member governments;

b) To examine, in the light of these interrelationships, housing finance policies in OECD countries with a view to identifying the objectives of major housing policies and programmes, with respect to cities, and innovative ways of achieving these objectives;

c) To examine, in particular, the role of housing finance policies as an instrument for the regeneration of urban areas;

d) To review, more specifically, the taxation policics and financing mechanisms operating in Member countries with regard to investment in housing; and

e) To advise governments on policies and programmes for urban housing finance that are adapted to changing social and economic conditions, in the light of the objectives identified for housing policy.

Sixteen countries (1) of the OECD participated in the Project on Urban Housing Finance (2). The present report brings together the results of the project and is based on the information supplied by Member countries in 16 national reports on their urban housing finance systems; on two special studies -- Tax Policies and Urban Housing Markets based on a Seminar co-sponsored by the United Kingdom and the University of Glasgow in March 1985 (3) and a report on Housing Maintenance and Modernisation based on on-site visits to twelve cities in ten Member countries in 1985 (4) --; and on the results of a Seminar on Housing Investment and Urban Change, co-sponsored by the OECD and the Greek government in Athens in May 1986 (5).

## Structure of the Report

In the course of its work the Project Group has endeavoured to relate its terms of refernce to the major housing policy issues as they are perceived in Member countries. This approach is reflected in the organisation of this final report. Thus Chapter I describes the changing, social, economic and political context within which urban housing policies are having to be formulated. Chapter II looks at the ways in which these housing markets themselves have been changing in recent years. In Chapter III the first of four specific policy areas is examined, viz., policies towards owner occupiers. This is followed, in Chapter IV, by an analysis of the operation of housing loan finance markets. Chapter V considers policies towards the rental sectors, both public and private. Finally, Chapter VI deals with policies for reinvestment (6) in the housing stock.

In each policy area an attempt has been made to identify:

a) The main concerns of Member countries;

b) The policies which are presently used in response to these concerns; and

c) To propose policy initiatives that are appropriate for dealing with these concerns, now and in the future.

A distinctive feature of the approach adopted by the Project Group has been to analyse, wherever possible, the impact of policies at the urban level. Frequently decisions about national policies are taken with little regard for their spatial implications. Yet if urban regeneration is to be successful, it is clearly important to devise a set of national policies that are compatible with it. To highlight this often neglected link, this report has tried to emphasize the relationship between national -- frequently supposedly non-spatial -- policies and their urban ramifications.

## NOTES AND REFERENCES

1. The Member countries which prepared national reports were: Australia, Canada, Finland, France, Germany, Greece, Japan, Luxembourg, the Netherlands, New Zealand, Portugal, Spain, Sweden, Turkey, the United Kingdom and the United States.

2. The officers elected by the project participants were chair, Dr. Claude Hemmer (Luxembourg), and vice-chairs, Dr. Eugen Dick (Federal Republic of Germany) and Dr. Dimitris Emmanouil (Greece).

3. "Tax Policies and Urban Housing Market", OECD, Paris, 1986. (Derestricted document, free on request.)

4. "Maintenance and Modernisation of Urban Housing", OECD, Paris, 1986. (Derestricted document, free on request.)

5. "Housing Investment and Urban Change", Proceedings of an OECD/Greece Seminar, OECD, Paris, 1988. (Derestricted document, free on request.)

6. The term "reinvestment" has been used by the Project Group to refer to the range of maintenance, modernisation and rehabilitation expenditures undertaken on the existing housing stock.

Chapter I

## THE CONTEXT OF HOUSING POLICY:  RECENT TRENDS
## AND PROSPECTS FOR THE FUTURE

In formulating their policies towards the housing sector, governments have to take account of a range of economic, social and political factors which both determine the nature of a country's housing requirements and the government's freedom of manoeuvre in attempting to meet them.

## A. The Macro-Economic Situation

The rate of growth of GDP and personal incomes will determine both the amounts of housing that individual households are able to afford through private expenditure and the amounts available to governments for public expenditure programmes. As such the macro-economic situation plays a key role in influencing housing policy. Moreover, the way in which the distribution of national income between households changes in response to macro-economic developments will also have implications for government income maintenance programmes, including those designed to enhance the ability to pay for housing.

The macro-economic environment within the OECD countries covered in this report has been subject to some abrupt changes over the last two decades. During the mid-70s, the prolonged post-war period of general economic stability and sustained economic growth came to an end. Substantial increases in oil prices in 1973-74 and then again in 1979-80 exerted severe contractionary pressure on the world economy. At the same time, the inflationary shocks represented by these price increases -- together with escalating wage costs -- led many countries to introduce restrictive macro-economic measures. These circumstances produced two periods of deep international recession in the mid-70s and in 1980, interspersed by a period of slow growth.

Table 1 presents some key macro-economic indicators which demonstrate the scale of the change in circumstances pre and post 1973-74. To do this it divides the period 1964-82 into two sub periods, 1964-73 and 1974-82, and indicates the annual average rates of growth of GDP, of unemployment, inflation and of real interest rates, by country, for each period.

All countries experienced a substantial slow down in the rate of GDP growth between the two periods. This applied across the range from the highest growth economy, Japan, where the rate fell from 8.8 to 3.8 per cent, to the lowest growth rate economy, the United Kingdom, where it fell from 3.3

to 0.8 per cent. The simple unweighted average growth rate of the 16 OECD countries covered by this report fell from 5.4 to 2.3 per cent.

The reductions in growth in output were reflected in increased rates of recorded unemployment. Once again, these were experienced by all countries: from Canada, which was at the top of the range with unemployment rising from 4.7 to 7.6 per cent, to Germany, where it rose from 0.8 to 3.6 per cent. Overall, the unweighted average for those of the 16 countries for which standardised unemployment rates are available, more than doubled from 2.3 to 5.4 per cent.

A particular feature of the post 1973-74 period was the simultaneous existence of historically high levels of unemployment and price inflation. Table 1 indicates the extent of price inflation and shows that the unweighted average increased from 5.5 to 13.9 per cent between the two periods. In many countries, however, nominal interest rates did not adjust fully in line with price inflation, with the result that real interest rates actually fell. In the housing market, it is the long term interest rate that is usually relevant and, as Table 1 shows, this fell quite steeply in some countries: notably Canada, France, Sweden, the United Kingdom and the United States. In Canada, New Zealand, Sweden and the United Kingdom the average real rate was actually negative over the period 1973-80.

Thus the macro-economic context within which housing policy has had to operate in the second half of the 70s and the early 80s has been one of modest growth in national output, high levels of unemployment and price inflation, but low rates of real interest. More recently, however, the situation has changed yet again. There has, in most countries, been a marked fall in the rate of price inflation. In 1985, the average rate for the 16 countries (excluding Greece, Portugal, Turkey and New Zealand where the rates were still high) was only 4.8 per cent. Once again, though, long term interest rates have been slow to adjust; this time, with the result that the long term real rate is now very high by historic standards. Rates of economic growth have started to pick up but unemployment remains stubbornly at high levels (see Table 2).

Prospects for the remainder of the decade and into the 90s are obviously difficult to predict. However, current OECD short term predictions suggest that the 40 per cent fall in the dollar price of oil imports which took place between 1985 and 1986 can be expected to have a favourable effect on both growth rates and price levels. Over the next couple of years GDP in OECD countries is forecast to rise at about 3 per cent per year, whereas the average rate of price inflation is expected to fall to approximately 3 per cent. The long term real rate of interest has started to fall in a number of countries, but its level remains high by earlier standards. Moreover, the increasingly close relationship between domestic interest rates and foreign exchange rates suggests that there is still potential volatility in this direction. Finally, there is no prospect of a dramatic improvement in the rates of unemployment. In many countries, the rate has continued to rise throughout the 80s and there is little indication that it will fall below an OECD average rate of 7 per cent in the foreseeable future.

Table 1

SELECTED MACRO-ECONOMIC INDICATORS, 1964-82

| | Average Annual Growth of GDP (a) | | Average Unemployment (b) | | Inflation Rate (c) | | Real Long-Term Interest Rates | |
|---|---|---|---|---|---|---|---|---|
| | 1964-73 | 1974-82 | 1964-73 | 1974-82 | 1964-73 | 1974-82 | 1967-73 | 1973-80 |
| Australia | 5.5 | 2.4 | 1.9 | 5.4 | 5.8 | 11.5 | - | 0.9 |
| Canada | 5.7 | 2.3 | 4.7 | 7.6 | 3.9 | 9.9 | 2.3 | -0.4 |
| Finland | 5.1 | 2.8 | 2.3 | 4.7 | 6.3 | 12.3 | - | 0.9 |
| France | 5.5 | 2.5 | 2.2 | 5.5 | 4.6 | 11.5 | 2.3 | 0.4 |
| Germany | 4.5 | 1.7 | 0.8 | 3.6 | 3.7 | 5.0 | 2.8 | 2.9 |
| Greece | 7.7 | 2.7 | - | - | 3.9 | 18.6 | - | - |
| Japan | 8.8 | 3.8 | 1.2 | 2.0 | 6.0 | 8.5 | 1.0 | 1.1 |
| Luxembourg | 4.9 | 0.8 | - | - | 3.7 | 7.6 | - | - |
| Netherlands | 5.4 | 1.5 | 1.5 (1) | 6.2 | 5.7 | 6.9 | 0.2 | 0.5 |
| New Zealand | 3.8 | 1.0 | - | - | 6.7 | 14.6 | -2.1 | -3.5 |
| Portugal | 7.2 | 3.0 | - | - | 6.4 | 22.4 | - | 4.9 |
| Spain | 6.5 | 2.0 | 1.4 | 8.4 | 7.4 | 17.4 | 1.5 | -0.9 |
| Sweden | 3.8 | 1.5 | 2.0 | 2.1 | 5.1 | 10.3 | - | - |
| Turkey | 5.8 | 5.5 | - | - | 9.4 | 42.1 | - | - |
| United Kingdom | 3.3 | 0.8 | 3.2 | 6.9 | 5.7 | 14.7 | 2.3 | -2.9 |
| United States | 3.5 | 1.8 | 4.4 | 7.1 | 3.8 | 9.0 | 1.1 | 0.3 |
| | | | | | | | | |
| Total of above (d) | 5.4 | 2.3 | 2.3 | 5.4 | 5.5 | 13.9 | 1.3 | 0.3 |

(a) Average annual percentage change at market prices.
(b) Percentage of total labour force.
(c) Average annual rate of increase in consumer prices
(d) Simple unweighted averaged.

1. Based on the years 1969-73 only.

Source: OECD Economic Outlook, OECD, Paris, May 1986.

Table 2

SELECTED ECONOMIC INDICATORS, 1983-86
(Annual Rates Percent/Year)

| | Growth of Real GNP/GDP in the OECD Area (% changes from previous period) | | | | Unemployment Rates in OECD Countries, commonly used definitions | | | | Consumer Prices | | | |
|---|---|---|---|---|---|---|---|---|---|---|---|---|
| | 1983 | 1984 | 1985 | 1986 | 1983 | 1984 | 1985 | 1986 | 1983 | 1984 | 1985 | 1986 |
| Australia | 0.4 | 7.2 | 5.5 | 1.5 | 9.9 | 8.9 | 8.2 | 8.0 | 10.1 | 3.9 | 6.8 | 9.1 |
| Canada | 3.2 | 6.3 | 4.3 | 3.3 | 11.8 | 11.2 | 10.5 | 9.6 | 5.9 | 4.3 | 4.0 | 4.2 |
| Finland | 3.0 | 3.3 | 3.5 | 2.4 | 5.4 | 5.2 | 5.0 | 5.5 | 8.3 | 7.1 | 5.9 | 3.6 |
| France | 0.7 | 1.4 | 1.7 | 2.0 | 8.4 | 9.9 | 10.2 | 10.5 | 9.6 | 7.4 | 5.8 | 2.7 |
| Germany | 1.9 | 3.3 | 2.0 | 2.5 | 8.2 | 8.2 | 8.3 | 8.0 | 3.3 | 2.4 | 2.2 | -0.2 |
| Greece | 0.4 | 2.8 | 3.0 | 1.3 | 8.3 | 8.3 | 8.0 | 7.6 | 20.2 | 18.5 | 19.3 | 23.0 |
| Japan | 3.2 | 5.1 | 4.7 | 2.4 | 2.6 | 2.7 | 2.6 | 2.8 | 1.9 | 2.2 | 2.1 | 0.4 |
| Luxembourg | 3.2 | 5.5 | 2.9 | 2.3 | 1.6 | 1.7 | 1.6 | 1.4 | 8.7 | 5.6 | 3.1 | 0.3 |
| Netherlands | 1.4 | 3.2 | 2.3 | 2.4 | 15.0 | 15.4 | 14.2 | 13.2 | 2.8 | 3.3 | 2.3 | 0.2 |
| New Zealand | 4.5 | 5.3 | 0.8 | 1.0 | 5.6 | 4.8 | 3.9 | 4.6 | 7.4 | 6.2 | 15.4 | 13.2 |
| Portugal | -0.3 | -1.6 | 3.3 | 4.3 | 8.3 | 9.0 | 9.2 | 9.2 | 25.5 | 29.3 | 19.2 | 11.7 |
| Spain | 1.8 | 1.9 | 2.2 | 3.4 | 17.7 | 20.6 | 21.9 | 21.5 | 12.2 | 11.3 | 8.8 | 8.8 |
| Sweden | 2.4 | 4.0 | 2.2 | 1.3 | 2.9 | 2.6 | 2.4 | 2.2 | 8.9 | 8.0 | 7.4 | 4.3 |
| Turkey | 3.3 | 5.9 | 5.1 | 8.0 | 16.1 | 16.1 | 16.3 | 15.6 | 28.8 | 45.6 | 45.0 | 34.6 |
| United Kingdom | 3.3 | 2.7 | 3.6 | 3.3 | 11.3 | 11.5 | 11.6 | 11.8 | 4.6 | 5.0 | 6.1 | 3.4 |
| United States | 3.6 | 6.8 | 3.0 | 2.9 | 9.6 | 7.5 | 7.2 | 7.0 | 3.2 | 4.3 | 3.5 | 2.0 |
| Average | 2.3 | 3.9 | 3.1 | 2.8 | 9.5 | 9.0 | 9.4 | 8.7 | 10.1 | 10.3 | 9.8 | 7.6 |

Source: OECD Economic Outlook, OECD, Paris, December 1987.

In devising housing policies during the second half of the 70s and early 80s, governments have, therefore, faced a number of macro-economic constraints. Notably:

-- A tightening of the availability of funds resulting from modest rates of GDP growth and anti-inflation policies;

-- An uncertain monetary environment in which both nominal and real interest rates have varied considerably;

-- High levels of unemployment which have limited the ability of a substantial minority of households to afford housing of an acceptable minimum quality without some form of subsidy payment.

For the future, the anticipated improvement in economic growth rates can be expected to provide the majority of the population with increasing income levels. This should enable private expenditure on housing to grow in line with household needs. At the same time, though, the persistence of high rates of unemployment will mean that continued subsidisation will be necessary for those households with limited purchasing power.

Modest rates of economic growth and concern over excessive public expenditure: GDP ratios can be expected to continue to exert restraint on the growth of public expenditure programmes. Given the increased demands emanating from large scale unemployment and other sources, this suggests that high priority housing objectives will only be able to be met within the budget constraint if policies are designed with greater regard to selectivity and targeting than has been the case in the past.

The monetary environment and the course of interest rates is likely to continue to pose problems. During the 70s lending institutions in a number of countries adjusted to high and volatile nominal interest rates through the adoption of new lending practices. Some of these remain relevant for future needs. But the problems of, particularly, the initial costs of owner occupation with high real interest rates will need to be dealt with. Moreover, high real interest rates are already having an adverse effect on the supply of housing in some countries such as Germany.

Finally, the feedback from housing policy to the macro-economic environment should not be overlooked. Current OECD advice to Member countries stresses the importance of speeding up the adjustment to structural change as a means of increasing economic growth. Increased labour market flexibility is identified as a key component in this process. Housing policy has a part to play in this process in so far as it contributes to greater labour mobility. More generally, housing policy will have a key role to play in the revitalisation of urban economies and can thereby contribute to overall economic growth.


B. Demographic Factors

Practically all of the OECD countries covered by this report have experienced a slow down in the rate of total population growth since 1960 (see Table 3). By the second half of the 70s, the annual rate of growth in the majority of Northern European countries had fallen to 0.5 per cent or below.

In Greece, Japan, New Zealand and the United States it had dropped to 1.0 per cent or below. Only in Turkey was population growing at over 2.0 per cent per year and only in Portugal did the rate of growth rise temporarily.

Table 3

TOTAL POPULATION: ANNUAL AVERAGE PERCENTAGE CHANGES, 1960-86

|  | 1960-67 | 1967-73 | 1973-80 | 1981-86 |
|---|---|---|---|---|
| Australia | 2.0 | - | 1.3 | 1.4 |
| Canada | 1.9 | 1.3 | 1.2 | 1.1 |
| Finland | 0.6 | 0.2 | 0.3 | 0.5 |
| France | 1.2 | 0.8 | 0.4 | 0.4 |
| Germany | 1.0 | 0.7 | -0.1 | -0.2 |
| Greece | 0.7 | 0.4 | 1.0 | 0.5 |
| Japan | 1.0 | 1.3 | 1.0 | 0.7 |
| Luxembourg | 0.9 | 0.9 | 0.5 | 1.1 |
| Netherlands | 1.3 | 1.1 | 0.7 | 0.5 |
| New Zealand | 2.0 | 1.4 | 0.8 | 0.8 |
| Portugal | 0.1 | -0.2 | 1.4 | 0.7 |
| Spain | 1.0 | 1.1 | 1.0 | 0.5 |
| Sweden | 0.7 | 0.6 | 0.3 | 0.1 |
| Turkey | 2.5 | 2.5 | 2.2 | 2.2 |
| United Kingdom | 0.6 | 0.3 | - | 0.1 |
| United States | 1.4 | 1.1 | 1.0 | 1.0 |
| Average | 1.2 | 0.9 | 0.9 | 0.7 |

Sources: OECD Historical Statistics, 1960-80, OECD, Paris, 1982.
OECD Main Economic Indicators, OECD, Paris, January 1988.

The principal determinant of the slow down in these rates of population growth has been the reduction in crude birth rates. These do not, however, immediately transmit themselves into reduced housing requirements. In a number of countries, including Turkey, the Netherlands, Finland, New Zealand, Australia and the United Kingdom, the lagged effect of high birth rates in the past is still filtering through in the form of household forming age groups. Elsewhere, in countries such as Canada, France and Japan which have recently been through this transition, the full effects of changes in past birth rates have worked themselves through and demographically driven demand has now stabilised.

Furthermore, despite the widespread stabilisation in total population numbers, changing social arrangements and a consequent continued growth in rates of household formation have combined to maintain growth in housing needs. The tendency towards smaller household size has been a particularly important factor in this respect (see Table 4). This trend is attributable to a number of developments. For example, there has been a marked increase in the numbers of elderly persons in most countries. Moreover, there has been a tendency for many of the elderly to seek greater independence in separate dwellings and, sometimes, specialised forms of housing. In addition, changing social customs have also led to the earlier and more extensive formation of young, single person households; to increases in the number of never married persons; and to greater numbers of single parent families.

Table 4

AVERAGE NUMBER OF PERSONS PER HOUSEHOLD,
SELECTED YEARS, 1970-85

| | Urban Population (U)/<br>Total Population (T) | 1970 | 1975 | 1980 | 1985 |
|---|---|---|---|---|---|
| Australia | T | | | | 2.8 |
| Canada | T | 3.6 | 3.2 | 2.9 | - |
| Finland | U | 2.9 | 2.7 | 2.5 | 2.4 |
| | T | 3.2 | 2.9 | 2.7 | 2.6 |
| France | U | 2.6 | 2.5 | - | |
| | T | 3.3 | 3.2 | - | |
| Germany | T | 2.8 | 2.6 | 2.5 | 2.4 |
| Greece | U | 3.2 | 3.1 | - | - |
| Japan | U | 3.6 | 3.3 | 3.2 | - |
| Luxembourg | | - | - | - | - |
| Netherlands | T | 3.3 | 3.1 | 2.9 | 2.7 |
| New Zealand | T | 3.4 | 3.4 | 3.0 | - |
| Portugal | Lisbon | 3.3 | - | 2.8 | - |
| | Oporto | 3.7 | - | 3.4 | - |
| Spain | T | 3.8 | - | 3.5 | - |
| Sweden | | - | | 2.3 | - |
| Turkey | T | 5.5 | 5.7 | 5.2 | - |
| United Kingdom | | - | - | - | - |
| United States | | - | - | - | - |

Source: OECD Project Group on Urban Housing Finance: Synthesis Report on National Position Papers, OECD, Paris, 1986.

The changing pattern of housing needs represented by these trends towards smaller household size may pose problems of adjustment in markets where the mass of housing services are provided by the existing stock of dwellings. Moreover, in the future, they will not only require changes in the size and design of new construction, but also changes in some of the established tenure and finance arrangements. This latter consideration is likely to be particularly pressing in those countries where the private rented sector -- which has traditionally housed large numbers of small households -- has experienced a decline in recent years.

The migration of population is also a potential source of changing housing needs. Within a country, the time taken for housing supply to adjust to changes in demand can mean that movements of population will place stress on some local markets while vacancies and excess supply exist elsewhere. Most OECD countries have experienced these pressures in the past as the substitution of capital for labour in agriculture led to substantial migration from rural to urban areas. This form of migration is now of less significance in the majority of countries, although it remained high until quite recently in Finland, Greece and Japan, and is still a source of urban housing problems in Portugal and Turkey.

Industrial restructuring and the relocation of industry has been a recent source of regional migration in a number of countries including Germany and the United States. In both these cases, there has been a movement from the older, Northern industrial areas to the growing regions of the South. These migration patterns have sometimes led to housing stress in the growing regions and decline in the regions suffering out migration. Similar economic causes and effects are also observable in the case of inner city to suburban migration.

External migration continues to play an important part in the growth of housing need in several countries. In Greece, the scale of repatriation has been sufficiently large to offset the effect of a falling population in the household forming age groups. External migration gains and losses of population have also been important, until recently, in Australia and Luxembourg, and are a continuing source of changing housing needs in New Zealand.

To summarise, it is likely that demographic factors will continue to exert a strong influence upon housing needs in the future. These will not, however, result from increases in the total population but rather from its changing composition and locational requirements.

C. The Urban Context

At the urban level, governments have also been faced with a series of new challenges. During the 50s and 60s, the high rates of national economic growth experienced by most OECD countries were based on industrial development centered on large urban areas. As a consequence, these areas experienced in-migration and grew as centres of employment, population and housing. In the 70s, however, reduced rates of economic growth and industrial restructuring have led to the decline of many of these urban areas. New forms of industry are no longer looking for locations within established urban areas and in countries such as Germany and the United States are shifting to new and growing regions. Older cities are, therefore, seeing an erosion of their industrial bases with a consequent loss of jobs and incomes. In a period of very high national rates of unemployment, the rates in these older cities have tended to be systematically above the national rate with particular concentrations among the young and, where they exist, ethnic minority groups.

However, the decline has not been distributed evenly across these urban areas. The particular decline of inner city manufacturing employment and the tendency for new jobs to be located in the suburbs, together with the preference of middle and upper income groups for suburban housing, has resulted in a distinct inner city problem. This is characterised by concentrations of social and economic deprivation: low income households living in poor housing conditions within a deteriorating environment. In countries such as Germany, the Netherlands, the United Kingdom and the United States, ethnic minorities, immigrants and guestworkers tend to be heavily concentrated in these areas where the older housing stock is the only housing which is accessible to them. There are also disproportionately large numbers of single person households -- both young and elderly. Hence there is a clear pattern of social segregation between the inner city and the suburbs.

While income levels within cities generally, and within inner cities in particular, have been restricted by these social and economic developments, the need for additional finance for housing and infrastructure reinvestment in these areas has become more pressing. The long term neglect of repair and maintenance work in both the public and private sectors has meant that much of the inner city housing stock is in a serious state of disrepair. Also, in some countries, large areas of public or social housing on the outskirts of cities have suffered similar neglect and consequent deterioration in quality. When public funds for reinvestment expenditure have been made available from central government revenues, they have been subject to the same tightening of budget constraints that has affected public expenditure generally. Sometimes, though, these funds are provided from local government revenues. In these cases, there has sometimes been an additional restriction arising from the erosion of city tax bases following migration to the suburbs.

In recent years, the special difficulties of urban areas have started to lead to the development of specifically urban regeneration programmes. But in most countries such programmes are still in their infancy. Given the deep seated nature of these urban problems, considerable emphasis will need to be placed on the design of these programmes in the future. A number of aspects that will require attention can be identified at the outset. First, there is the basic problem of information. Far too little is known about the linkages between different forms of housing investment and urban regeneration. Second, it needs to be recognised that the majority of economic and social policies are formulated at the national level with little regard for their urban implications. Sometimes these can have adverse consequences at the local level. Third, the continuing pressure on public funds suggests that, in many countries, efforts will need to be made to attract greater quantities of private finance into the reinvestment process. The amounts of private sector finance that, through leverage, a given sum of public expenditure can produce, may need to become a relevant public sector investment criterion.

Of course, not all OECD countries have experienced this process of urban decline. In the Federal Republic of Germany a market approach to housing has been adopted. This has included the liberalisation of rent legislation. As a result of these policies, there are few maintenance and modernisation problems and great progress has been made with renewal schemes in those areas where they have been needed.

In those countries with less mature economies, and in selected regions in all countries, substantial migration from rural to urban areas, and from smaller to larger urban areas is continuing to take place. This may pose a variety of problems. In Turkey, the arrival of substantial numbers of low income households into urban areas with insufficient purchasing power to buy or rent good quality accommodation has led to the growth of large areas of sub-standard illegal squatter housing. This was also a problem for Greece in the past, but now the problem is more one of unplanned illegal building in general. Both Spain and Portugal also have the task of providing adequate housing for low income, recent arrivals to urban areas. The task for these countries is to manage urban change and subsidisation within tightening budget constraints.

## D. Political and Administrative Considerations

To a large extent, socio-demographic trends, changes in the macro-economic environment and many of the developments affecting urban areas are all exogenous factors which have all exerted a strong, deterministic impact upon housing policies. But it would be wrong to imply that policies have been determined solely by external constraints. In all countries governments have been able to exert a degree of choice. It is the interplay of constraints and choices based upon political values that has produced the sets of housing policies found in OECD countries.

There is, of course, a spectrum of political values among OECD countries and this gives rise to different forms of institutional arrangements. At the most general level there are different perceptions about the appropriate role of government. In some countries the prevailing view is that government should restrict its role to the provision of an environment within which the market system can operate as the primary means of allocating resources. This approach is based on a belief in the superior efficiency of the market. Government intervention will sometimes be necessary to remove or overcome specific sources of market failure, and also for modifying the market distribution of income, but it will occupy a subsidiary role. In other countries there is less confidence in the efficiency of the market and/or a greater relative importance attached to the equity of the income distribution. This tends to lead to more widespread government intervention. Some idea of the range of political differences in outlook between OECD countries is provided by looking at the ratio of government spending-to-GDP (see Table 5). Fairly clearly, the view of government in Sweden -- where the ratio is over 60 per cent -- is far more interventionist than in, for example, Australia, Japan or the United States.

While the total public expenditure/GDP ratio provides an index of the degree of total government involvement within individual countries, it does not indicate the fact that most governments have tended to intervene more extensively in the housing market than most other ones. This is because of the special characteristics associated with housing. The basic need for shelter, the extreme durability of housing, external costs and benefits associated with its use and the extremely high price: income ratio of this commodity have all led to the formulation of specific housing policies.

Notwithstanding this emphasis, the late 70s and 80s have been significant for the extent to which governments in a number of countries have sought to reduce the size of the public sector and thereby increase the scope for goods and services to be provided by the private sector. In pursuing this aim, numerous privatisation schemes have been introduced across a whole range of economic and social policies. And despite its special characteristics, the housing market has not been excluded from these developments. The encouragement of owner occupation and the deregulation of housing capital markets are the two most widespread examples of reductions in the role of government. On the other hand, though, other countries have been less influenced by these trends, and have continued to favour a strong government presence in the housing sector, often using it as an explicit instrument of social, employment or regional policy.

Table 5

TOTAL OUTLAYS OF GOVERNMENTS AS A PERCENTAGE OF GDP, 1983-85

|  | 1983 | 1984 | 1985 |
|---|---|---|---|
| Australia | 38.1 | 38.7 | 38.5 |
| Canada | 46.9 | 47.0 | 47.0 |
| Finland | 40.3 | 39.9 | 41.5 |
| France | 52.0 | 52.7 | 52.4 |
| Germany | 48.3 | 48.0 | 47.2 |
| Greece | 38.2 | 40.2 | 43.8 |
| Japan | 34.1 | 33.2 | 32.7 |
| Luxembourg | 54.6 | 50.6 | - |
| Netherlands | 62.2 | 61.3 | 60.2 |
| New Zealand | 38.1 | 38.7 | 38.5 |
| Portugal | - | - | - |
| Spain | 38.8 | 39.3 | 42.2 |
| Sweden | 66.2 | 63.5 | 64.5 |
| Turkey | 30.9 | - | - |
| United Kingdom | 48.1 | 48.9 | 47.7 |
| United States | 36.9 | 35.8 | 36.7 |

Source:   OECD Economic Outlook, OECD, Paris, December 1987.

Chapter II


AN OVERVIEW OF HOUSING MARKETS AND HOUSING POLICIES


A. The Stock of Dwellings and its Condition

The size of the dwelling stock, by country, for the most recent years
for which data are available is shown in Table 6. In the past the traditional
concern in most OECD countries has been to ensure that the total supply of
dwellings is adequate to provide for the accommodation needs of all
households. However, while this is still a concern in countries such as
Portugal, Turkey and, to a lesser extent, the Netherlands, the majority of
countries have now achieved a balance or an aggregate net surplus of dwellings
over households. Clearly, this reflects the success of policies geared
towards the achievement of quantitative housing targets.

In assessing the adequacy of the supply of housing, though, it should
be borne in mind that the number of households is not always independent of
the number of dwellings. To some extent, separate households tend to form as
dwellings become available. Hence rates of household formation and the demand
for housing are supply constrained. Account also needs to be taken of the
vacancy ratio and the incidence of second homes. In the United Kingdom, for
example, older areas of social housing tend to have high vacancy rates; there
are also high general vacancy rates in lower quality housing in Japan.
Furthermore, variations in demand and supply between areas may mean that local
excess demand and excess supply exist simultaneously in different areas. This
is, of course, a particular problem for urban housing markets as these are the
areas in which excess demand is most likely to be concentrated. (Table 6
shows the degree of urbanisation in Member countries in terms of the
percentage of dwellings and of population found in urban areas. The
concentration of dwellings in urban areas tends to be greater than that of
population, reflecting smaller urban household sizes. These figures should,
however, be treated with caution because of the different definitions of urban
areas adopted by different countries).

Notwithstanding these qualifications about the interpretation to be
placed on these aggregate dwelling and household numbers, most countries have
increasingly turned their attention towards the issue of housing quality. One
of the best measures of housing quality is per capita floorspace.
Unfortunately no figures are available on an internationally comparable
basis. In their absence, Tables 7 and 8 assemble some of the available data
on housing conditions. As far as dwelling size is concerned, Canada and New
Zealand are at the top of the range with an average of 5/6 rooms per
dwelling. Luxembourg, the Netherlands and the United Kingdom also have a

large average dwelling size with 5 or more rooms. Turkey -- which has the smallest average dwelling size -- has suffered from a critical shortage of supply in the past, but this is now beginning to improve. As is to be expected, average dwelling sizes tend to be smaller in urban than in rural areas. The density of occupation ranges from 0.5 to 0.9 persons per room. Interestingly, where data are available, there is no systematic evidence of higher densities of occupation in urban compared with rural areas.

Interior housing conditions -- as indicated by the availability of water facilities -- vary somewhat between countries and facilities. The basic level of provision of inside running water is high, especially in urban areas. In all countries, 90 per cent or more dwellings have this facility. The level of provision of inside flush toilets is similarly high in most countries although Japan is a notable exception with less than 50 per cent of its dwellings possessing this facility (1978 data). There is also a markedly higher incidence of this facility in urban areas. The percentage of dwellings possessing a fixed bath or shower tends to be rather lower than in the case of the other two facilities, but in most countries over 80 per cent of dwellings have the facility.

In many cases the quality of a dwelling is closely correlated with its age. Given this association, it is relevant to note the incidence of older housing in established, industrialised countries. In Northern Europe, for example, the percentage of the dwelling stock constructed before 1949 in five of the Member countries is as follows: Germany (36.5 per cent), France (44 per cent), the Netherlands (32.7 per cent), Luxembourg (41.8 per cent) and the United Kingdom (51 per cent). The substantial numbers of older housing in these and other countries are recognised as a source of major concern. In the United Kingdom there is a serious problem of cumulative disrepair in both the public and private sectors. Despite recent efforts on modernisation, Luxembourg also has a problem of declining quality in the rental sector. A similar problem exists in the United States where spatial concentrations of deteriorating low cost housing have resulted from a combination of the filtering process (see page 46 for a more full description of this process), legal restrictions and market imperfections. In the Netherlands, supply limitations and unacceptably high densities among older housing continue to give cause for concern. Clearly the problems of ageing and qualitative decline in substantial parts of national housing stocks are widespread.

However, although the problems of housing deterioration are widespread, they are not universal. Canada, Australia and New Zealand all have comparatively recently built housing stocks and do not yet have a major reinvestment problem. Also high standards of building construction technology used in countries such as Sweden and Finland have also kept the problem to minimal proportions.

Finally, on the subject of housing quality, the quality of the environment is obviously of importance too. In this connection, the provision of adequate infrastructure remains a problem in Greece, Portugal, Japan and Turkey. In areas of informal housing it is particularly difficult and expensive to install infrastructure services after development has taken place. To overcome this problem, there is a need for more clearly developed and binding forms of land use planning.

Table 6

TOTAL NUMBERS OF DWELLINGS AND HOUSEHOLDS, 1981-85
(Millions)

| | Total Dwellings | Percentage of Dwellings in Urban Areas | Households | Definition of Urban Area | Percentage of Population in Urban Areas (d) |
|---|---|---|---|---|---|
| Australia | 4.7 (1981) (a) | - | 4.7 (1981) (a) | 100 000 | 69 |
| Canada | 8.8 (1981) (a) | 84.0 (1981) (b) | 8.3 (1981) (a) | 10 000 | 51 |
| Finland | 1.8 (1980) (b) | 64.7 (1980) (b) | 1.8 (1980) (b) | 10 000 | 53 |
| France | 23.7 (1978) (c) | 74.6 (1975) (b) | - | 100 000 | 46 |
| Germany | 26.8 (1984) (a) | - | 25.3 (1982) (a) | 100 000 | 33 |
| Greece | - | - | - | - | - |
| Japan | 38.6 (1983) (a) | 78.8 (1978) (b) | 35.2 (1983) (a) | 5 000 | 76 |
| Luxembourg | 0.1 (1981) (c) | - | - | - | 100 |
| Netherlands | 5.3 (1985) (a) | - | 5.4 (1985) (a) | - | 100 |
| New Zealand | 1.0 (1981) (b) | - | - | - | 61 |
| Portugal | - | - | - | 30 000 | 32 |
| Spain | 14.6 (1980) (e) | 67.8 (1981) (a) | 10.7 (1981) (a) | 10 000 | 73 |
| Sweden | 3.5 (1980) (b) | 85.7 (1980) (b) | 3.5 (1980) (b) | 500 000 | 30 |
| Turkey | 8.6 (1980) (a) | 15.7 (1975) (b) | - | 10 000 | 45 |
| United Kingdom | 21.5 (1983) (a) | - | - | 10 000 | 78 |
| United States | 91.7 (1983) (a) | - | 88.4 (1980) (a) | 50 000 | 62 |

Sources:  (a)  OECD Group on Urban Housing Finance, National Position Papers.
          (b)  U.N. Compendium of Human Settlement Statistics, UN, New York, 1985.
          (c)  Eurostat, Yearbook of Regional Statistics, Office of the European Communities, Brussels, 1985.
          (d)  OECD Group on Urban Housing Finance, Synthesis Report of National Position Papers.
          (e)  U.N. Annual Bulletin of Housing and Building Statistics for Europe.

Table 7

DWELLING SIZES AND DENSITIES OF OCCUPATION, 1975-81

| | | | Rooms per dwelling | | | Persons per room | | |
|---|---|---|---|---|---|---|---|---|
| | | | Total | Urban | Rural | Total | Urban | Rural |
| Australia | | | - | - | - | - | - | - |
| Canada | (1981) | (b) | 5.6 | 5.5 | 6.1 | 0.5 | - | - |
| Finland | (1980) | (b) | 3.4 | 3.2 | 3.7 | 0.8 | 0.8 | 0.8 |
| France | (1975) | (b) | 3.4 | 3.3 | 3.7 | 0.8 | 0.4 | 0.8 |
| | (1978) | (c) | 3.7 | - | - | 0.8 | - | - |
| Germany | (1978) | (b) | 4.4 | - | - | - | - | - |
| | (1978) | (c) | 4.2 | - | - | 0.6 | - | - |
| Greece | (1981) | (a) | 3.4 | 3.3 | 3.6 | 0.9 | 0.9 | 0.9 |
| Japan | (1978) | (b) | 4.3 | 4.1 | 5.1 | 0.8 | 0.8 | 0.7 |
| Luxembourg | (1981) | (c) | 5.3 | - | - | 0.5 | - | - |
| Netherlands | (1977) | (b) | 5.0 | - | - | - | - | - |
| | (1977) | (c) | 5.0 | - | - | 0.6 | - | - |
| New Zealand | (1981) | (b) | 5.6 | - | - | 0.5 | - | - |
| Portugal | | | - | - | - | - | - | - |
| Spain | (1980) | (a) | 4.9 | 4.9 | 5.1 | 0.7 | 0.8 | 0.7 |
| Sweden | (1980) | (b) | 4.1 | 4.1 | 4.4 | 0.6 | 0.6 | 0.6 |
| Turkey | (1975) | | 2.5 | 2.5 | 2.5 | - | - | - |
| United Kingdom | (1980) | (b) | 5.0 | - | - | 0.6 | - | - |
| United States | (1980) | (b) | 4.7 | - | - | 0.6 | - | - |

Sources: (a) OECD Group on Urban Housing Finance, National Position Papers
(b) U.N. Compendium of Human Settlement Statistics, UN., New York, 1985.
(c) Eurostat, Yearbook of Regional Statistics, Office of the European Communities, Brussels, 1985.
(d) OECD Group on Urban Housing Finance, Synthesis Report of National Position Papers.

Table 8

SELECTED INDICATORS OF HOUSING CONDITIONS, 1976-81

Percentages of dwellings with the following inside the dwelling:

| | Running water | | | Flush toilet | | | Fixed bath or shower | | | Central Heating |
|---|---|---|---|---|---|---|---|---|---|---|
| | Total | Urban | Rural | Total | Urban | Rural | Total | Urban | Rural | Total |
| Australia (1976) (b) | 97.1 | - | - | 92.2 | - | - | - | - | - | - |
| Canada (1981) (b) | 99.5 | 99.8 | 97.5 | 98.9 | 99.5 | 96.1 | 98.8 | 99.6 | 95.1 | - |
| Finland (1980) (b) | 90.6 | 95.2 | 82.7 | 85.5 | 92.7 | 73.1 | 70.0 | 78.2 | 55.6 | - |
| France (1975) (b) | 97.2 | 98.4 | 93.7 | 71.9 | 7.9 | 54.5 | 70.3 | 75.8 | 54.1 | - |
| (1978) (c) | 99.2 | - | - | 85.0 | - | - | 84.7 | - | - | 67.5 |
| Germany (1978) (b) | - | - | - | 97.1 | - | - | 89.2 | - | - | - |
| (1978) (c) | 99.2 | - | - | 92.5 | - | - | 89.1 | - | - | 63.7 |
| Greece | 92.7 | 95.0 | 84.5 | 45.9 | 54.2 | 15.7 | - | - | - | - |
| Japan | - | - | - | - | - | - | 82.8 | 80.1 | 92.8 | 72.9 |
| Luxembourg (1981) (c) | 100.0 | - | - | 95.8 | - | - | 84.9 | - | - | 57.2 |
| Netherlands (1977) (c) | 100.0 | - | - | 99.9 | - | - | 87.6 | - | - | - |
| New Zealand | - | - | - | - | - | - | - | - | - | - |
| Portugal | - | - | - | - | - | - | - | - | - | - |
| Spain (1980) (a) | 96.2 | - | - | 92.4 | - | - | 83.0 | - | - | 8.5 |
| Sweden (1980) (b) | - | - | - | 96.2 | 98.7 | 82.1 | 93.1 | 95.7 | 78.1 | - |
| Turkey | - | - | - | - | - | - | - | - | - | - |
| United Kingdom (1981) (c) | 100.0 | - | - | 96.0 | - | - | 97.0 | 95.7 | 78.1 | 61.0 |
| United States | - | - | - | - | - | - | - | - | - | - |

Sources: (a) OECD Group on Urban Housing Finance, National Position Papers.
(b) U.N. Compendium of Human Settlement Statistics, UN, New York, 1985.
(c) Eurostat, Yearbook of Regional Statistics, Office of the European Communities, Brussels, 1985.

## B. Investment in Housing

The extent to which quantitative and qualitative housing objectives can be met obviously depends largely upon the levels of investment in the sector. The main determinant of the availability of resources for investment expenditure on housing -- both private and public -- is the rate of growth of national income. In most countries, the steady rates of economic growth prior to 1973/74 were accompanied by similar, or even higher, rates of growth in housing investment. But since then slower rates of growth have been mirrored by reductions in the levels of housing investment (see Table 9). This dampening of investment activity did not solely arise from reductions in levels of aggregate demand. On the cost side, the rate of increase in land prices and construction costs both exceeded the rate of growth in prices generally and thereby served to raise the relative price of new building (see Table 10). And, of course, high levels of real interest rates also exerted a strong influence in a sector with high interest rate sensitivity.

Table 9

ANNUAL GROWTH RATES OF GROSS PRIVATE RESIDENTIAL
FIXED CAPITAL FORMATION, 1967-86 (Per Cent/Year)

|                | 1967-73 | 1974-79 | 1980-86 |
|----------------|---------|---------|---------|
| Australia      | 8.0     | 0.8     | 0.8     |
| Canada         | 7.7     | 3.6     | 4.2     |
| Finland        | 7.7     | 0.2     | -1.0    |
| France         | 7.2     | 2.0     | -3.0    |
| Germany        | 3.0     | -1.1    | -1.5    |
| Greece         | 11.9    | 4.6     | -5.8    |
| Japan          | 15.0    | 0.4     | -1.2    |
| Luxembourg     | -       | -       | -       |
| Netherlands    | 7.1     | -0.9    | -0.9    |
| New Zealand    | 5.7     | -8.1    | 3.6     |
| Portugal       | -       | -       | -       |
| Spain          | 7.3     | -3.5    | -0.6    |
| Sweden         | 1.4     | -0.9    | -1.3    |
| Turkey         | -       | -       | -       |
| United Kingdom | 5.2     | 0.4     | 1.5     |
| United States  | 7.5     | 2.0     | 3.8     |

Source:    OECD Economic Outlook, OECD, Paris, December 1987.

In fact, these reductions in gross private investment expenditure possibly even understate the reductions in the growth of housing provision in recent years. This is because in many countries there was an increase in the number of single or two-family homes at the expense of multi-family dwellings. In Germany, for instance, the share of single family homes among newly constructed dwellings rose from about 40 per cent between 1970 and 1974 to approximately 70 per cent between 1978 and 1980. A similar trend was

28

observable in France. Thus, because single family homes tend to have higher standards and construction costs, the number of newly built dwellings increased even less slowly than total investment expenditure.

Table 10

ANNUAL CHANGES IN CONSUMER PRICES AND THE RESIDENTIAL
CONSTRUCTION IMPLICIT PRICE INDEX, 1960-82 (Per Cent/Year)

|  | Consumer Prices | Construction Prices |
|---|---|---|
| Australia | 6.7 | 7.5 |
| Canada | 6.1 | 6.7 |
| Finland | 8.2 | 9.5 |
| France | 7.1 | 8.1 |
| Germany | 4.1 | 5.9 |
| Greece | 8.7 | 10.6 |
| Japan | 7.1 | 6.6 |
| Luxembourg | 4.7 | 6.9 |
| Netherlands | 5.7 | 7.8 |
| New Zealand | 8.4 | - |
| Portugal | 11.4 | 12.4 |
| Spain | 11.0 | 14.6 |
| Sweden | 6.9 | 7.9 |
| Turkey | 19.7 | 17.1 |
| United Kingdom | 8.9 | 9.6 |
| United States | 5.5 | 5.8 |

Source:  OECD Group on Urban Housing Finance, Synthesis of National Position Papers.

These reductions in the levels of housing investment expenditure had the most noticeable effect upon the construction of new dwellings, since repair, maintenance and modernisation activity (i.e. reinvestment) actually increased quite significantly. As a result its relative share in housing investment has increased in most countries. As well as representing a direct response to the problems of deteriorating quality described previously, this shift of emphasis has the advantage of promoting a labour intensive activity with favourable employment generating effects. It also reduces the inputs of land and materials in comparison with new construction.

Despite reductions in the scale of investment expenditure on housing in recent years, it has been argued by some commentators that there has still been excessive investment in this sector in comparison with other sectors of the economy. Those holding this view maintain that favourable tax treatment of housing and the individual household's desire to invest in an asset where "real" values are maintained during inflationary periods has led to over-investment. The case is made particularly with reference to owner occupation. A detailed consideration of this claim and the evidence relating to it is presented in Chapter III.

29

## C. Tenure Distribution of the Housing Stock

The durability and high price-income ratio of housing means that it is almost unique among those goods and services purchased directly by final consumers in having substantial sectors of both user owned and rented dwellings. Moreover, the rental sector is notable for the existence of large numbers of social or public housing in several countries.

Attitudes towards the different forms of tenure tend to vary between countries (see Chapters III and V), although, in the majority of them, owner occupation is viewed favourably both by individual households and by governments. Reflecting this preference, the proportion of households within the owner occuped sector rose steadily throughout the 70s in most countries. Rising real disposable incomes of those in employment and negative real interest rates assisted the process. It also received considerable support from governments in the form of subsidy and tax expenditure incentives. The levels of owner occupation reached in the period 1980-85 are shown in Table 11. In all but four countries the percentage of owner occupiers was well in excess of 50 per cent, and in Australia, New Zealand, Greece and the United States it was around 70 per cent.

Table 11

TENURE DISTRIBUTION OF THE HOUSING STOCK, 1978-85

| Year | | Urban/ Total | Owner Occupied | Rental | | | Other |
|------|---|------|------|------|------|------|------|
| | | | | Public (1) | Private | Total | |
| 1981 | Australia | T | 71.0 | 5.3 | 17.6 | 22.9 | 6.1 |
| 1981 | Canada | T | 63 | 4 | 33 | 37 | - |
| 1980 | Finland | U | 62 | - | - | 38 | - |
| 1982 | France | U | 40 | - | - | 51 | 9 |
| 1978 | Germany | T | 37 | - | - | 63 | - |
| 1982 | Greece | U | 60 | - | - | 40 | - |
| | | T | 72 | - | - | 28 | - |
| 1983 | Japan | T | 62 | 8 | 24 | 32 | - |
| 1981 | Luxembourg | T | 65 | - | - | 35 | - |
| 1985 | Netherlands | T | 45 | 37 | 18 | 55 | - |
| 1980 | New Zealand | T | 71 | 6 | 23 | 29 | - |
| 1981 | Portugal | T | 56 | 4 | 35 | 39 | 4 |
| 1980 | Spain | T | 67 | - | - | 24 | - |
| 1985 | Sweden | T | 42 | 23 | 20 | 43 | 15 |
| 1979 | Turkey | U | 59 | 3 | 29 | 32 | 9 |
| 1983 | United Kingdom | T | 60 | 31 | 9 | 40 | |
| 1980 | United States | U | 60 | - | - | 40 | - |
| | | T | 73 | - | - | 27 | - |

1. Includes cooperatives.

Source: OECD Group on Urban Housing Finance, National Position Papers.

Since 1980, rising real interest rates and the necessity for households further down the income scale to enter owner occupation, if its expansion is to be maintained, have acted as a dampening influence on the sectors growth in some countries. Elsewhere, though, the expansion has been boosted by special programmes; for example, the sale of substantial quantities of public housing to tenants at discount prices within the United Kingdom. Despite this programme, the United Kingdom is still notable -- along with the Netherlands and Sweden -- for its large stock of public housing.

## D. Government and Housing

All OECD governments subscribe to the basic housing objective of ensuring a decent home for every household, within a satisfactory local environment, at a price within its means. General statements of intent of this form contain four main elements in terms of which practical policies are formulated. First, there is the concern to ensure adequacy in the supply of housing. Second, to ensure that its quality reaches at least an acceptable minimum standard. Third, there is the desire to produce a satisfactory neighbourhood environment. And fourth, there is concern about the price of accommodation in relation to household incomes.

The actual policies and instruments which are used to meet these objectives vary between countries depending, as they do, on the existing state of national housing markets and the range of social, economic and political factors within which individual governments must operate. However, despite this diversity, it is possible to identify some broad categories of government policies which are used to a greater or lesser extent in all countries. For convenience, these may be categorised as policies on:

-- Regulation;

-- Subsidisation (both direct and indirect); and

-- Direct provision.

### Regulation

Regulatory policies usually involve a minimal amount of government involvement. The role of the government is restricted to the regulation of the way in which the private market operates through specific legal instruments; expenditure is usually limited to financing monitoring agencies. Two main forms of regulatory policy are found within housing markets in OECD countries: rent control and the regulation of housing finance markets.

Rent control was introduced in most countries as a short term measure designed to protect tenants from high market rents that would otherwise arise during periods of exceptional shortages of private rental accommodation. Frequently, however, controls have remained in force over considerable periods of time with adverse effects on the size and quality of the rental housing stock. In a number of countries, the rate of decline of the sector has been accelerated as better quality rental accommodation has been transferred to the owner occupier sector, leaving a shortage of suitable rented accommodation for those households normally housed in this sector. Current policy concerns centre on the need to provide assistance to tenants without deterring the supply of rental housing (see Chapter V).

Housing finance represents a rather different aspect of the housing market but, nonetheless, one where regulatory policies have been operated extensively. In most countries, governments have insulated the housing finance system from the general capital market and regulated the terms and/or cost on which credit is offered. In recent years, some countries have removed these restrictions in an attempt to make capital markets more competitive (e.g. United States, New Zealand, United Kingdom and Sweden). This has had consequences for the supply and cost of credit (see Chapter IV).

## Subsidisation

There is a whole spectrum of policy instruments through which governments reduce the price of housing paid by users below its full costs of production. These operate on both the supply and demand side of the market. On the supply side there are, for example, subsidies to private developers, non-profit housing associations, co-operatives and public housing agencies which enable them to let or sell their dwellings below their full cost. The actual subsidies are paid in a variety of ways, either directly or indirectly: through direct cash grants, low interest loans, or tax exemptions and allowances.

On the demand side, there are a number of ways in which governments subsidise the housing expenditure of rental tenants. Rent subsidies, housing allowances and vouchers are all used. In choosing between them, governments need to decide on the relative advantages of cash payments versus earmarked allowances, the form of income taper to use if they are income related, the type and quantity of housing on which they are made available, etc. (see Chapter V).

Many countries offer demand side subsidies to owner occupiers in the form of low interest loans. But possibly more importantly, there are the indirect subsidies offered to them in the form of tax expenditures. In the majority of countries, owner occupiers receive substantial amounts of assistance through tax exemptions and allowances on certain items of housing expenditure. At the present time, there is a good deal of concern about the efficiency, equity and escalating costs of these programmes, with numerous consequent calls for their reform (see Chapter III). Apart from these general subsidies, recent interest in reinvestment has led to a series of subsidies to owners which are related specifically to repair, maintenance and improvement expenditure (see Chapter VI).

## Direct Provision

In practically all countries governments have taken responsibility for the direct provision of at least part of the housing stock. This may involve direct construction by public sector agencies, but more usually it is undertaken by the government acting as a developer and sub-contracting the actual construction work to private sector firms. The dwellings built in this way may be sold (either complete or semi complete as one of the Luxembourg programmes allows), or maintained and managed as rental housing by the government or one of its agencies. In recent years, many governments have taken an active role in direct provision through "buyout" strategies associated with urban reinvestment programmes (see Chapter VI).

Current policy debates associated with publicly provided housing tend to focus on its relative cost in relation to other forms of housing assistance; its method of finance, especially the levels at which rents are set; and the ways in which the stock of housing is managed. In the latter connection, there is a general trend favouring the decentralisation of management functions. In addition, in some countries attention has been attracted to the serious deterioration in the quality of housing on certain large scale, public housing estates and to the tendency for them sometimes to become socially segregated with heavy concentrations of low income and/or ethnic minority households. Both France and the United Kingdom have experienced these trends, often on large estates built on the periphery of major cities.

Apart from the direct provision of housing by government in the ways described above, there are a diverse set of organisational forms through which governments can assist indirectly the provision of housing. In Greece, for example, the government has been active in assisting the establishment of non-profit, housing cooperatives.

The extent to which governments within individual countries intervene in their housing markets in the various ways described above is summarised in Table 12. This shows some of the main policy instruments used for regulation (credit control), subsidisation (public lending, tax subsidies, etc.), and direct provision (construction) and the relative levels of government intervention in each case.

## E. Current Policy Issues

The housing sector has certain special features which distinguish it from other sectors of the economy. Notable among these are the extreme durability of housing; the existence of widespread externalities associated with its use; and its very high price-income ratio compared with most other consumer goods. It is these features that have led to its particular form of market structure and constitute the context within which major policy concerns have arisen in recent years.

Durability and high price income ratios have led to the growth of two distinct forms of tenure: owner occupation and renting. In most countries the distinction between tenures represents an important consideration in the formulation of policy. This may be because the encouragement of owner occupation is considered desirable; or because there is concern over the relative costs to governments of subsidising each sector. The rising relative costs of housing and the problem of consumers' ability to afford it have brought this issue to the forefront of the policy agenda. Moreover, the dependence of housing on specialised loan finance and the ways in which the financing instruments employed by lending institutions have been affected by changes in the macro economic environment have led governments to become involved in influencing the operation of loan finance markets.

Table 12

LEVELS OF GOVERNMENT INVOLVEMENT IN THE HOUSING SECTOR

| | Credit Control | Public Lending | Subsidisation | Construction |
|---|---|---|---|---|
| Australia | M | L | M | L |
| Canada | L | L | H | L |
| Finland | H | H | H | H |
| France | H | M | H | M |
| Germany | M | M | H | H |
| Greece | H | L | H | L |
| Japan | M | H | M | L |
| Luxembourg | H | L | L | L |
| Netherlands | M | H | H | H |
| New Zealand | L | M | L | L |
| Portugal | L | L | M | L |
| Spain | M | L | M | M |
| Sweden | H | H | H | M |
| Turkey | H | L | M | L |
| United Kingdom | M | L | H | H |
| United States | L | L | H | L |

Key:  H = High;  M = Medium;  L = Low

Source:  OECD Group on Urban Housing Finance, Synthesis Report of National Position Papers.


The durability of housing, and the external costs and benefits to which it gives rise, has posed special problems associated with its ageing and depreciation. These have been of particular concern where they are concentrated spatially in urban areas and have led to the formulation of a range of urban reinvestment strategies.

The importance of these aspects of housing in all OECD countries -- and the emergence of a number of special policy problems associated with them in recent years -- led the Project Group on Urban Housing Finance to select them as topics for special investigation. Accordingly, the four main chapters of the report deal with:

-- Policies towards owner occupiers;

-- Housing loan finance institutions and instruments;

-- Policies towards the rental sector;

-- Housing reinvestment strategies

## F. The Urban Dimension

The ways in which urban areas have been subjected to new pressures in recent years have already been referred to in Chapter I. Industrial restructuring and the movement of jobs and population; the economic decline of inner city areas; and the problems of deteriorating urban housing stocks are all issues with which many of the older industrialised countries are seeking to cope. In the more recently industrialising countries, rapidly growing urban areas and shortgages of housing and infrastructure continue to pose problems. However, despite numerous urban investment initiatives in recent years, no country has a coherent, specifically urban, housing finance policy. In most cases, housing policies are formulated and implemented by central governments on a national rather than an urban or regional basis. Even when, say, the administration and ownership of public housing is decentralised, as in the United Kingdom, the funding of programmes is closely controlled by central government. Similarly high levels of Federal government control over finance are found in the United States, Australia and Canada.

The dominance of central governments and national policies has led to a serious neglect of the urban implications of many housing policies. Frequently decisions about national policies have been taken with little regard for their spatial implications. This is particularly regrettable as it is the urban housing market that so often represents the point of confluence of numerous, disparate housing policies and processes. To illustrate, the extensive debate about the incidence and effects of housing tax expenditures rarely considers the impact that they are likely to have had on urban areas in particular. And yet if urban regeneration strategies are to be given a high priority on the policy agenda, it is clearly inefficient to pursue them within the context of incompatible, supposedly non spatial, national policies.

Of course, many of the policy issues chosen for special investigation in this report are of importance on a national basis aside from their urban consequences. But a distinctive feature of this report is that their urban implications are considered alongside these wider considerations.

Chapter III

## POLICIES TOWARDS OWNER OCCUPIERS

A range of objectives towards owner occupation are found among the OECD countries participating in the Urban Housing Finance Project.

At one end of the spectrum there are governments, such as that of the United Kingdom, which view owner occupation as desirable per se and are actively encouraging its expansion. In recent years statements by governments of each of the main political parties have emphasized the desirability of owner-occupied housing. The current government would prefer to see a greater proportion of housing, particularly new housing in the owner-occupied or private rented sector than in the social rented sector. The government's view is that home ownership encourages self help, individual responsibility and social stability. As such it makes an important contribution to the enterprise culture upon which a successful free market economy depends.

In a slightly different category, there are a number of countries which -- while actively encouraging the expansion of owner occupation -- are doing so for more pragmatic reasons of housing policy. In Germany and Japan, for example, the expansion of owner occupation is seen as the most efficient means of ensuring growth in the supply of good quality housing. Thus it is the objective of housing supply rather than tenure which is paramount. At the same time, it is claimed that lower administrative costs and the extensive use of owners' labour in repair and maintenance work -- which is probably valued less highly than priced labour -- mean that both the real resource costs of owner occupation and its costs to the public sector are lower than in the case of rental housing. Furthermore the benefits of the spread of owner occupation are held to extend beyond home buyers themselves as their vacated dwellings tend to filter down to lower income groups who are thereby able to increase the quality of their housing.

In a third category, there are those countries where owner occupation is viewed favourably, and where it is the majority form of tenure, but where current government policies are not aimed primarily at its further general expansion. In the United States, for example, government policy is designed to increase the role of the private market in the supply of housing in the belief that a market system will produce a more efficient allocation of resources. However, this approach extends to the private rental sector as well as owner occupation. Similarly, both Australia and New Zealand have levels of owner occupation that are very high by international standards (c.70 per cent), but have recently abolished certain tax policies which favoured owner occupiers. France and Canada also provide examples of countries where there is a general consensus in favour of owner occupation, but where recent policies involve changes which suggest a rather greater degree of neutrality in the treatment of different tenure groups.

The aim of tenure neutrality -- that is, a policy stance which aims to treat households equivalently whatever their housing tenure group -- is a feature of the approach favoured by a fourth set of countries. Both Sweden and the Netherlands subscribe to this aim. As a result, the stock of public sector rental housing in these countries tends to be high by international standards.

Finally, there are those countries with less mature economies where the immediacy of housing supply objectives coupled with limited ability of households to pay for housing have led to large scale public sector investment programmes. Thus in Greece there has been a call for increased public expenditure on social housing. In Turkey the government favours a similar approach in response to the problem of inadequate, urban squatter housing, although more recently increased reliance has been placed on the private rental sector. In Portugal, a government planning system has been utilised to respond to the challenge of housing shortages and reduced ability to pay. These experiences suggest that although the growth of owner occupation -- as a strategy for increasing and improving the housing stock -- may be suited to countries with relatively high income levels, elsewhere a more varied strategy may be necessary. This may require the mobilisation of resources by the public sector in the face of limited private purchasing power.

Clearly, as the above examples demonstrate, objectives concerning owner occupation vary between OECD countries. But notwithstanding these elements of diversity, all countries offer substantial subsidies to owner occupiers, either as part of the general subsidisation of all housing or as particular incentives to owner occupation. The remainder of this chapter examines these subsidy arrangements. In particular, it considers:

-- The instruments that are used for subsidy purposes;

-- The effectiveness of these instruments in terms of housing market objectives and, in particular, their consequences for urban housing markets;

-- Some proposals for improving the effectiveness of housing subsidy programmes.


SUBSIDY INSTRUMENTS


Two main forms of subsidy to owner occupiers are found in OECD countries: direct subsidies in the form of low interest loans for house purchase, and indirect subsidies in the form of tax concessions to home owners.

A. Low Interest Loans

The servicing of mortgage debt constitutes the major item of housing expenditure for most owner occupiers. This burden is particulary demanding in the early years of a mortgage loan when the repayments-to-income ratio is typically at its highest. Subsidies which reduce the rate of interest payable by the borrower to below the market rate of interest represent a direct response to this problem. As such, these subsidies are used widely as a means of improving access to owner occupier housing. Moreover, in recent years many countries have developed interest rate subsidy programmes which incorporate targeting features designed to meet specific housing or related objectives. These features typically define the eligibility for a loan, and vary its amount and cost, according to specified dwelling or household characteristics. The following examples, which are not intended to be exhaustive, illustrate some of the main features of interest rate subsidy schemes found in Member countries.

In Japan, the Housing Loan Corporation provides long term low interest loans to both prospective buyers and private developers supplying housing for sale. The loans are restricted to housing meeting certain design requirements (e.g. size, structure, etc.), and larger loans are offered on dwellings incorporating desirable features such as energy saving devices. In this way the subsidy system can be used to exert influence on the quality of housing being built. There is also targeting towards individuals as preferential loan terms are offered to households with aged or handicapped members. In recent years, the increasing cost of the programme, at a time when public expenditure constraints have tightened, has led to the introduction of income restrictions on the recipients of low interest loans. At the same time, the amount of subsidy any household receives is now progressively reduced after a number of years via the adoption of "stepped" interest rates. These become operative from the 11th year of the loan when the initial burden can be expected to have been reduced.

Germany also offers low interest loans on the basis of the borrowers income level. They are, however, restricted to newly constructed dwellings. Households with relatively low incomes -- who gain little from tax relief -- are assisted in this way. Under the primary promotion scheme, which is more intensive in terms of subsidisation, beneficiaries receive public building loans amounting to, on average, DM 60 000-DM 80 000 at subsidised interest rates as well as degressive expenditure subsidies based upon the amount of floor space. Under the so-called secondary promotion scheme, for which 40 per cent higher income limits apply, the intensity of subsidisation is lower. People wishing to build in agglomerations can receive loans based upon floor space up to a specified maximum amount. This relief is reduced over a period of 15 years.

The selection of households is made by the local authorities taking the income limit for publicly assisted housing and the number of children into account. There is no legal claim to assistance. Most of the funds go to rural areas because the acquisition of owner-occupied property is easier for lower-income households there. Accordingly, in communes with less than 50 000 inhabitants 5.3 per cent of the housing stock is accounted for by publicly assisted owner-occupied dwellings while the corresponding figure for cities with more than 200 000 inhabitants is only 2.2 per cent.

The Housing Corporation of New Zealand -- which is the largest single lender in the country with slightly under one third of the market -- makes most of its low interest loans on the security of new dwellings. There are also income limits on borrowers and a requirement that borrowers provide a percentage of the purchase price from their own resources.

In Sweden, 99 per cent of the purchasers of new housing qualify for a direct loan from the National Housing Board. This covers up to 30 per cent of the cost. Once a state loan has been obtained, borrowers qualify for priority loans from private housing finance institutions which cover up to 70 per cent of the costs. Until very recently the housing finance institutions obtained their funds through the sale of bonds at rates of interest that were negotiated by the government at a little below the market rate. Other financial institutions were obliged to purchase certain quantities of these bonds. In this way, the supply of funds was guaranteed at below market rates. (However the priority market for housing bonds was abolished in December 1986.) In practice, a number of countries have effectively offered subsidies to borrowers in a similar fashion, through the regulation of mortgage interest rates. Through regulation, the rate charged to borrowers is kept below the rate it would be in a free market; in this case, however, the subsidy does not come from the government (or taxpayers) but from the depositor who receives a below market rate of interest from housing savings and loan institutions.

Other aspects of targeting that are found in Member countries include: allocation by household size (Finland and France); by region (Greece and Finland); and by the organisation of the applicants e.g. cooperatives, the self employed, etc. (Turkey). Interest subsidies have also been used as temporary measures in periods when mortgage costs have risen dramatically in the face of steeply rising interest rates. Hence, in Canada, the Canada Mortgage Renewal Plan (1981) offered assistance to households whose mortgage costs exceeded 30 per cent of their gross income. The scheme was discontinued for new applicants in 1983.

B. Tax Expenditures

A tax expenditure is usually defined as a departure from the generally accepted tax structure which produces favourable treatment of particular types of activity or groups of taxpayers. It may take the following forms: tax exemptions, where income from particular sources is excluded from the tax base; tax allowances, which are sums deductible from gross income in order to arrive at taxable income; tax credits, which are sums deducted directly from tax liabilities, and which may exceed tax liabilities; and finally, rate reliefs, where specific types of activities or taxpayers are subject to reduced rates of tax.

Tax expenditures are an important source of housing subsidy in practically all OECD countries, even though they do not always appear in public expenditure accounts. Indeed one of the main ways in which central governments have assisted this sector has been through its tax treatment. In France, Germany and the United Kingdom, for example, tax expenditures represent approximately 50 per cent of the total fiscal subsidy received by the housing sector. It is often the case, however, that the system of housing tax expenditures has emerged as the tax system has evolved rather than being specifically designed to meet specific housing policy objectives. At the present time five main forms of housing tax expenditure exists; these offer exemptions, allowances or rate reliefs on:

-- Mortgage interest payments and imputed income;

-- Wealth and capital gains;

-- Property taxes;

-- Sales taxes;

-- Income from savings schemes.

## Mortgage Interest Payments and Imputed Income

The treatment of interest payments and/or income under normal principles of taxation may take one of two approaches. Under the first of these, owner occupier housing is treated as an investment good producing imputed rental income which is liable to taxation. If this is the case, certain costs incurred in the purchase and upkeep of the asset are deductible from gross income for tax purposes. The second approach treats owner occupier housing as a consumer good. In this case, it is not liable to income tax but, under normal principles, the owner may not deduct outgoings for tax purposes. Tax expenditures are measured in terms of the departures from these normal principles, depending on whichever applies in a particular country (see Table 13).

In the countries shown in Group A in the table the investment approach to owner occupier housing is applied: that is, the imputed rental income is liable to taxation. In these countries, therefore, the deduction of outgoings, especially loan interest payments, does not constitute a tax expenditure since it represents an application of the normal tax principles to investment income. Rather, it is the undervaluation of imputed rental income which tends to lead to owner occupier property being taxed less heavily than other forms of investment, and which constitutes the main form of tax expenditure.

Rental valuation is usually carried out through an administrative procedure and expressed in terms of a flat percentage of the capital value of the property. This percentage ranges from between 1 and 4 per cent depending on the country. However, unless property valuation is kept under permanent review, administratively defined values tend to lag behind market values. This is, of course, a particular problem in periods when property prices are changing rapidly. Furthermore, in those countries where total outgoings, including those in excess of the rental value, may be set against non-housing income, there is considerable scope for reducing overall tax payments. For these reasons, some countries have simply abandoned the practice of taxing the rental value of owner occupier property (e.g. the United Kingdom and France) whereas others have set limits on the deduction of loan interest or housing costs (e.g. Germany and Spain).

A more numerous set of countries appear to adopt the consumer good approach to owner occupier housing in the sense that no tax is levied on the imputed rental income (Groups B and C). However, a number of these countries also permit the interest payments on loans for house purchase or construction to be deducted from income for tax purposes (i.e. Group B). This represents an investment good approach to outgoings and, thereby, clearly violates the normal tax practice towards consumer goods. In the case of these countries, considerable tax expenditures are received by owner occupiers: these may be measured in terms of the absence of imputed income tax or the gains accruing from interest rate deductibility. Of the countries covered in this report, only Australia, Canada and New Zealand operate a fully consistent consumer good, tax policy.

40

Table 13

THE INCOME TAX TREATMENT OF OWNER OCCUPIER HOUSING

| Group A | Group B | Group C |
|---------|---------|---------|
| Finland | France | Australia |
| Greece | Japan | Canada |
| Luxembourg | Portugal | New Zealand |
| Netherlands | Turkey | |
| Spain | United Kingdom | |
| Sweden | United States | |
| Denmark | Federal Republic of | |
| Norway | Germany | |

Group A: Countries which tax imputed rental income and allow tax deductions on loan interest payments.

Group B: Countries which do not tax imputed rental income but allow tax deductions on loan interest payments or housing costs.

Group C: Countries which do not tax imputed rental income nor allow tax deductions on loan interest payments.

Source: OECD Group on Urban Housing Finance, National Position Papers.

Where mortgage interest payments are tax deductible, the deduction may be offered in two main ways. The most common practice is to offer a tax allowance whereby loan interest is set against gross income. If the income tax schedule is progressive, this means that the higher the household's income, the greater the tax benefit. It also means that no benefit accrues to those households whose incomes are too low for them to be liable to taxation. Alternatively, as in France, for example, a credit is set against the households marginal tax rate. With this arrangement it is also possible for payments to be made to low income households whose credit exceeds their tax bill.

Targeting of income tax expenditures takes a number of different forms. In most countries they are confined to the owner's main residence, although in some countries, e.g. the United States they extend to second homes. The amounts of tax relief may be restricted by stipulating a maximum size of loan on which interest deductibility may be made, as in the United Kingdom; or the proportion of the loan interest on which it is obtainable, as in Japan; or by restricting tax concessions to the early years of the loan, such as the first five years as in France, or to eight years in total from the time of purchase as in Germany. They may also be restricted to once in the borrower's lifetime, as in Germany or be related to family size, as in France and Germany. Few countries restrict them to only low income groups. Recently, increased attention to energy conservation has led a number of countries to target tax incentives towards energy savings schemes. The United States, France, Germany and the Netherlands are all among the countries which have offered tax concessions for insulation and other energy saving work.

41

## Wealth and Capital Gains

In practically all countries wealth held in the form of owner occupier housing, and the capital gains realised through its sale, are exempt from taxation. There are, however, a number of conditions attached to these exemptions. Most countries restrict exemption to the owner's main residence, although in France it extends to second homes. There are also conditions relating to reinvestment in housing. In the United States, for example, capital gains on the sale of the taxpayer's main residence are not liable to tax provided that the taxpayer purchases a new residence during the following two years, and that the purchase price is not less than the sale price of the previous dwelling. If the second condition is not met, capital gains tax is charged on the difference between the sale price and the purchase price. Similar arrangements apply in Japan. In the United Kingdom, exemption from capital gains tax is subject to a continuous residency requirement; that is, the dwelling must have been used continuously for owner occupation since its purchase, otherwise tax is payable on part of the capital gain. Canada imposes similar conditions. The two countries which provide the main exceptions to wealth and capital gains tax exemption are Sweden, where nominal capital gains over the first four years of residence are subject to taxation and real capital gains from the fifth year; and the Netherlands, where an annual wealth tax applies and housing is included in the wealth tax base.

## Property Taxes

In most countries tax concessions are given to owner occupiers in the form of property tax exemptions, reductions in the property tax base or the tax rate. Thus both Germany and Japan offer reductions in the tax base ranging from 11 to 75 per cent; the United Kingdom and Australia offer reduced rates of tax on residential property; whereas in the Netherlands and Japan small and low valued units are exempt from property taxation. In New Zealand, housing is also exempt from property taxation if it is owned by non-profit making associations, 75 per cent of whose capital is held by the residents.

In a number of countries property tax concessions are specifically targeted at new housing construction. For example, new property is exempt from tax for two years after construction in France. In fact, this exemption may be extended to 15 years when the property is the taxpayer's main residence and it has been subsidised by a government means-tested loan. Similar schemes offer full or partial exemption in Germany (for 10 years after construction), Japan (3 years), Spain (3 years) and Turkey (5 years).

## Sales Taxes

The sales tax treatment of housing construction differs widely across OECD countries reflecting the diversity of indirect tax structures. In general, housing construction is liable to central or local government sales taxes, although these are often applied differentially in this sector. Hence, in EEC Member countries and in Sweden and Turkey, housing transactions are, in principle, subject to value added tax (VAT). But there are many departures from normal VAT procedures. In France, for example, VAT on purchases of land for building is payable after a 30 per cent reduction in the tax base; this reduces the real rate from approximately 18 to 13 per cent. Also, in France,

housing sales by low cost housing associations and local authorities are VAT
exempt when they are financed by government-subsidised, means-tested loans.
In the United Kingdom the sale of both new and existing housing is zero rated
for VAT Purposes.  In Luxembourg, on the other hand, there is no VAT exemption
for housing.


Income from Savings Schemes

Special schemes designed to assist households in saving for home
ownership have been introduced in a number of countries in recent years.
Through these schemes, savings receive preferential treatment for tax
purposes: either through tax free interest and bonuses, or the deduction of
savings deposits from taxable income.  Countries offering such schemes include
Australia, Canada, Finland, France, Germany, Japan, Luxembourg, the
Netherlands, New Zealand and Portugal.  Two countries which place particular
emphasis on savings schemes -- Canada and Germany -- provide illustrations of
the ways in which typically they work.

Registered home ownership savings schemes are the main form of
assistance for home ownership in Canada.  These are contractual schemes, which
were introduced in 1974, aimed at facilitating saving for the necessary
downpayment for a purchase of a first home.  The contracts have a maximum
maturity of 20 years and may be taken out with banks, credit institutions and
investment trusts.  They must be registered with the tax administration.
Interest on deposits is tax free (subject to a maximum deposit contract of
($10 000) and deposits are deductible in full from total taxable income.
Finally, there is provision for "clawing back" the tax expenditures if the
savings are not actually used for purchasing housing at the end of the period.

Subsidised savings schemes also play a major role in Germany.
Households wishing to purchase housing may take out a savings contract with a
specialised financial institution;  through this they undertake to make
monthly payments based on the amount of the contract and the intended savings
period.  These deposits currently earn 3 per cent per year.  When payments to
the value of 40 per cent of the contract have been made, the contract holder
may obtain a loan to the value of the other 60 per cent of the contract at an
interest rate of 5 per cent.  For low income households, subsidies from the
Federal government are available:  through bonus payments related to the
amount saved and the number of children in the household.  Bonus payments are
tax free.

Finally, on the question of owner occupiers' exemption from taxes, it
is worth noting that in some countries they are liable to taxes that are not
borne by renters.  These taxes can take the form of property taxes paid by
owners only (e.g. France) or transactions taxes paid at the time of purchase
or sale of a house (e.g. stamp duties in France and the United Kingdom).  To
some extent these taxes may offset tax expenditures offered to owners;
however, in most countries, they are not very significant.

THE EFFECTIVENESS OF SUBSIDIES TO OWNER OCCUPIERS

In the previous section the range of direct and indirect policy instruments used to subsidise owner occupier housing in OECD countries was described. In this section an assessment of the effectiveness of these instruments is presented. As a reflection of their greater quantitative importance, and the volume of the debate surrounding them, the sequence of the previous section has been reversed so that indirect subsidies -- that is, tax expenditures -- are dealt with first.

## A. Tax Expenditures

Many critics have argued that housing tax expenditure programmes as presently operated in the majority of OECD countries are inefficient, inequitable and have had a generally adverse effect upon urban housing markets. These criticisms have been levelled particularly at the tax exemption of imputed rental income and/or the allowances offered on mortgage interest payments.

### Efficiency

At the macro-economic level, one claim of inefficiency rests on the belief that by increasing the post-tax rate of return on investment in owner occupier housing vis-à-vis other investment goods, tax allowances and/or exemptions have led to an expansion of the housing sector at the expense of other areas of the economy. As the rate of productivity tends to be lower in the housing sector than elsewhere in the economy, this tax induced diversion of resources will have a detrimental effect upon the long run, rate of growth of national output. Moreover, it is argued that these effects have been accentuated during periods of inflation when, as is usually the case, tax systems have not been indexed for price changes. Hence the value of tax exemptions and allowances rise with inflation whereas the post-tax rate of return on non-housing assets is further reduced by the taxation of nominal income. In this way, tax induced distortions in relative rates of return are held to cause significant shifts in the pattern of investment across the national economy.

However, this interpretation of events is the subject of some dispute. At the most general level, resting as it does on the assumption that a perfectly competitive market would determine the optimal amount of housing investment, it ignores the fact that governments may actually choose to favour investment in housing for explicit social or political reasons. Secondly, empirical evidence on the subject is non conclusive. Evidence from Germany, for example, suggests that contractual savings schemes -- which are a major part of the housing finance system -- are to a large extent insulated from national finance markets and are not, therefore, likely to mobilise significant quantities of funds that would otherwise have flowed into money and equity markets. On the other hand, though, it is important to point out that the closer integration of housing finance circuits with equity and money markets, which has resulted from the deregulation of housing finance that has taken place in a number of OECD countries in recent years, may be expected to increase the probability of "crowding out".

Another reservation about the actual importance of crowding out concerns the source of housing investment funds. It may be that housing investment displaces consumption expenditure rather than savings/investment. Moreover, some countries point out that the major source of investment funds for large companies is retained profits and that these are unlikely to be affected by the rates of return to housing. Finally, the fact that in most OECD countries residential investment declined as a percentage of total fixed investments over the period 1973-85 has been cited as counter evidence to the crowding out hypothesis.

To summarise the crowding out debate, it seems that tax expenditures do provide an incentive for investment in housing at the expense of other forms of investment, but that they operate within an environment where there are many other influences at work. At the present time there is insufficient evidence to establish their precise effect. Opinions within Member countries do not suggest that they constitute a major source of resource misallocation between housing and non housing sectors.

Two rather more pragmatic criticisms of tax expenditures on efficiency grounds are that the revenue costs to the Exchequer have risen in a rapid and uncontrolled fashion; and that as instruments they are often poorly targeted given their underlying objective of increasing owner occupation and/or improving the quality of the housing stock.

The precise measurement of the cost to the Exchequer of tax expenditures is complicated by the existence of three alternative approaches. First, there is the "revenue forgone" approach: this measures the cost by comparing the revenue generated by the existing tax legislation with that which would arise in the absence of tax expenditures, on the assumption that there would be no change in taxpayers' behaviour. Second, there is the "revenue gain" approach: this is the same as the first approach except that it endeavours to take into account the behavioural responses of tax payers to the withdrawal of tax expenditures, including the secondary impacts of a changing tax structure on the overall level of economic activity. This consideration is particularly important if economic policy is geared towards supply side initiatives. Finally, there is the "equivalent outlay" approach. This is based on a calculation of the cost of replacing tax expenditures with direct expenditures such that the recipient's position remains unchanged as a result of the switch.

As all three of the above methods are used in OECD countries, comparisons between them are hazardous. Nonetheless, it is certainly the case that, whichever measure is employed, the costs of tax expenditures have risen significantly in practically all countries where they are offered. Moreover, this has usually taken place in an automatic rather than a discretionary manner -- largely as a result of inflation and rising interest rates. As such, it is a major cause of concern. Indeed, as the previous section showed, there have been a number of attempts to control escalating costs through the designation of various conditions and "ceilings" on eligibility for tax expenditures. Furthermore, as the revenue gain and equivalent outlay measures of cost suggest, the large sums devoted to tax expenditures can have important implications for government budgets and the more general health of the economy. For example, the removal of tax expenditures would enable governments to lower marginal tax rates, or raise direct expenditure levels, without any deterioration in overall budget deficits. Lower marginal tax rates may have favourable effects on the supply of labour through increased work incentives. Alternatively, higher direct expenditure programmes which exactly compensated for the increased tax receipts resulting from the withdrawal of tax expenditures may, through the balanced budget multiplier, create additional output and employment.

Whether or not tax expenditures are targeted efficiently depends upon the precise form of the tax system. However, in many countries there is only a loose link between the structure of tax expenditures and the pursuit of the expansion of owner occupation and improvement of the housing stock. In these countries tax expenditures are not administered in a cost effective way as the bulk of expenditure goes to existing owner occupiers long after they have entered the sector, rather than being directed at marginal households who are about to enter, or have recently entered, the sector. The main justification offered for this long term subsidisation is that it facilitates the spread of owner occupation and the upgrading of the housing stock through the filtering process.

Filtering takes place when better-off households move into newly constructed housing and vacate their previous dwellings which then become available for households lower down the income scale. To the extent that this sets in operation a chain of moves, it provides the opportunity for an improvement in the quality of housing obtained by in-movers at each stage in the chain. Thus the benefits of tax expenditures received by higher income, existing owners -- which encourage them to upgrade their housing demand -- have a "knock on" effect and thereby benefit lower income households further along the housing chain as better quality housing filters down the system.

Filtering has for many years been the subject of a policy debate concerning the most efficient way of improving housing standards, especially for low income groups. Some governments argue that the filtering process transmits benefits throughout the housing market and therefore favour tax expenditure programmes that rely upon it. Others claim that housing will not filter sufficiently far or fast to benefit those at the bottom of the housing chain. And certainly the limited empirical evidence does suggest that filtering chains "decay" very rapidly. Furthermore, even if some of the benefits are passed on from the original recipient of the tax expenditure, there is likely to be a considerable "leakage" in this process.

Given the uncertainty surrounding the efficacy of the filtering process, it is likely to be more cost effective to target tax expenditures at particular groups and/or in terms of specific housing objectives, rather than offering them across-the-board to all owner occupiers. As the previous section showed, a number of countries have done this. Schemes which restrict tax concessions to first time buyers and/or the period of time over which they are offered represent group specific targeting mechanisms, whereas tax concessions on energy saving expenditures provide examples of housing specific targets. Even in these cases, though, the normal absence of income restrictions on tax expenditure recipients means that some part of the tax concession may simply displace private housing expenditure which would have taken place anyway.

However, in addition to filtering, some governments may take the view that a general system of mortgage interest relief will encourage a more active housing market than would otherwise be the case, offering home owners a greater opportunity to geographical and social mobility than might be available if they were constrained by administrative arrangements to one particular area or type of housing. This may be particularly relevant in times when economic circumstances are changing the employment opportunities of different groups or in different regions of a country. In some countries which adopt a more targeted approach to the subsidisation of housing, difficulties may have been experienced in ensuring that sufficient mobility is possible to meet employment needs.

## Equity

Among housing economists and other specialists there is a widespread belief that tax exemptions on imputed rental income, and/or allowances on mortgage interest payments, as presently administered in most countries, are inequitable. This applies at both the horizontal and the vertical level.

Horizontal inequity arises because similar households receive different tax and subsidy treatment according to their housing tenure group. In particular, tax expenditures received by owner occupiers mean that for all but the lowest incomes households (who, in many countries, receive income related benefits when they are in the rental sector), the subsidies they receive as owner occupiers are higher than they would receive in the rental sector. This differential treatment may, of course, be part of a government's attempt to encourage owner occupation as a tenure group. Sometimes this may introduce a conflict between housing and more general equity objectives.

Vertical inequity occurs because the amount of tax expenditure a household receives tends to be positively related to its income. This "regressivity" arises for two main reasons. First, as the income elasticity of demand for housing is positive, higher income groups will demand more housing than lower income groups. As exemptions and allowances are related to the quantity of housing consumed and/or the size of the mortgage loan, these will also rise with income. Second, insofar as tax expenditures are applied to marginal rates of tax, they necessarily generate the largest proportionate and absolute subsidies to households which pay the higher tax rates. In addition, the regressivity of the overall distribution of tax expenditures is increased because the proportion of households that are owner occupiers -- and therefore receiving tax expenditures -- increases as one moves up a country's income distribution. Therefore, both the amount of tax expenditure received at a given income level, and the number of owner occupiers at that level, will rise as the level of income increases. However, part of the explanation of tenure choice depends upon the household's stage in its life cycle. Established households are more likely to be found in owner occupation than newly formed ones. A full assessment of the equity implications of tax expenditures should take account of the household's complete life-cycle experience.

Another issue that needs to be addressed when considering the distribution of housing tax expenditures is the distinction between their formal incidence and their effective incidence. Formal incidence refers to those households who are the legal recipients of the tax expenditures under the prevailing tax laws, whereas the effective incidence refers to the ultimate recipients of the benefits after all the economic effects have worked themselves out. In the housing context, this distinction centres on the potential capitalisation of tax expenditures into house prices. Through this process, additional demand facilitated by tax expenditures simply bids up the price of the existing stock of housing. In these circumstances, existing owners at the time of the introduction of a tax expenditure will benefit from a capital gain, but subsequent purchasers (who constitute the vast majority of owners in most countries) will not receive this benefit as they will have bought at post-capitalisation prices. Thus subsequent purchasers receive formal but not effective subsidies. (Subsequent purchasers will, however, receive some benefit <u>vis-à-vis</u> rental tenants as, on the eventual repayment of their mortgage loans, they will be in possession of an asset whose relative value has risen -- as a result of tax expenditures -- in relation to non-housing assets).

The extent of the capitalisation of tax expenditures into house prices depends crucially on the elasticity of housing supply. To take two polar extremes: if there is zero elasticity (i.e. the supply of housing is totally unresponsive to the tax expenditure induced increase in demand), there will be full capitalisation into house prices. At the other extreme, if there is infinite supply elasticity (i.e. a complete adjustment of supply), there will be no capitalisation. Clearly most countries lie somewhere between these two extremes. The question of time and the rapidity of adjustment is obviously a key one. Over what period of time can supply adjustment take place? It is well known that, in general, adjustment time lags in the housing market are far longer than in many other markets. The quantitative importance of the existing stock in relation to new construction, the limited scope for technical advance in the construction industry and the proliferation of planning laws in many countries all combine to produce adjustment lags. In specific circumstances the capacity of housing supply to respond to changes in demand will depend upon the availability of residential land and changes in this availability in response to changes in its price. The capacity to adapt the existing housing stock to new patterns of use will also be important. Overall, the extent of tax capitalisation will clearly depend on the success of these adjustment mechanisms and can be expected to vary between countries and, indeed, between areas within countries.

The latter point -- that is, differential supply elasticities within individual national housing markets -- raises another potential source of tax expenditure regressivity. As access to local job markets is important for low income groups, there is likely to be demand for dwellings in close proximity to urban centres where there are concentrations of low wage employment. Land for such dwellings is often in scarce supply. On the other hand, the dwelling location constraint is likely to be less binding for higher income groups who are more able to undertake commuting travel. Hence, in effect, the supply of dwellings is more elastic. This means that the distribution of effective tax expenditures will be even more regressive than the formal distribution.

## Urban Implications

Recently attention in a number of countries has turned towards the adverse consequences that national tax expenditure programmes have had upon urban areas. Suburban sprawl, social segregation and the erosion of inner city tax bases have all been cited as outcomes towards which tax expenditures have contributed.

During the 70s there was a substantial change in urban growth trends and patterns of urbanisation in the more industrialised countries of Western Europe and North America. Within these countries many of the established metropolitan areas lost their dominance as centres of economic activity.

Instead, the peripheral areas of these cities, and newly expanding cities in more prosperous regions, became centres of economic growth. In other countries, at an earlier stage of industrialisation and urbanisation, substantial migration from rural to established urban areas continued. In both cases, however, low density suburban housing development accompanied these trends.

The low density development represented by suburban sprawl imposes a number of economic and social costs. It may outstrip and impede the provision of publicly financed infrastructure, such as water and sewage facilities. This is a particular problem in countries such as Greece, Portugal and Turkey where substantial amounts of illegal development take place. Even when low density building is legal it tends to result in higher infrastructure unit costs. At the same time, there are often low levels of neighbourhood amenities and a deterioration in the environment resulting from the erosion of open spaces.

Suburbanisation can also have implications for the wider urban area by imposing costs on inner city residents when it results from the out migration of middle and upper income households. This is because it tends to produce a degree of social segregation between the central city and the suburbs with the inner areas having disproportionate numbers of low income and economically inactive households. These concentrations of deprivation are often a source of high levels of crime, ill health and other sources of social costs. Moreover, in those cities where the suburban development is outside of the city tax base, the scope for the local government to deal with these of demands on its budget will be limited as its revenue raising capacity will also be reduced.

To a large extent, these patterns of suburban housing development have followed the relocation of economic activity described above. Developments in transport technology and policy have also contributed towards it. However, in many countries, tax expenditures which encourage owner occupation have also been a contributory factor. For it has been in the suburbs that the majority of single family, owner occupier property has been built. Moreover, apart from the general correlation between the spread of owner oocupation and suburbanisation, the process of differential tax capitalisation described earlier provides a specific link between tax policies and suburbanisation.

Tax expenditures can be expected to increase the demand for housing but supply cannot always expand to meet this demand. As a result house prices will rise. However, the rate at which prices increase will vary across the urban area. In the suburbs, where building land is more plentiful and land use controls tend to be less restrictive, prices may be expected to rise less than in the inner city. Substantive empirical evidence on differential rates of price increase across urban areas is scare, but U.S. studies suggest that the price elasticity of new housing supply per unit of land ranges from approximately 0.9 in open suburbs to almost zero in the city centre. Thus middle and upper income households who have greater purchasing power and mobility will be attracted to the suburbs where their tax expenditures are able to buy more housing rather than be dissipated in higher prices. This may be expected to reinforce the tendency for suburbanisation resulting from the qualitative and environmental aspects of suburban housing having a high income elasticity of demand.

Finally, there is also a link between the encouragement of owner occupation in the suburbs and the decline in the quality of many areas of inner city housing which results from the relative tax treatment of acquisition and occupancy costs. Acquisition costs are those outlays which the purchaser incurs through buying a dwelling and include transaction costs, downpayments and mortgage interest payments. Occupancy costs are expenditures incurred while consuming the services of the dwelling and include utility charges, property taxes and repair and maintenance expenditure. There is considerable variation in practice across OECD countries, but where tax concessions are concentrated on acquisition costs, this is likely to be detrimental to the maintenance and improvement of the existing stock. In a spatial sense it is possible that tax expenditures have provided insufficient incentive for the repair and maintenance of older, inner city housing in comparison with new building in the suburbs and thereby contributed to inner city decline. This issue is dealt with more thoroughly in Chapter VI which deals with reinvestment policies.

## B. Low Interest Loans

In terms of their effects upon the allocation of resources, low interest loans share many of the general features of tax expenditures. That is, they encourage investment in housing in general, and owner occupation in particular, and also contribute to suburbanisation. Their main difference, though, on both efficiency and equity grounds, is that they are often targeted more precisely. This has been undertaken in order to meet specific equity and housing objectives, but also for the more pragmatic reason that low interest loans would otherwise attract substantial excess demand and therefore some form of rationing device would be necessary.

In the majority of countries this targeting has been operated in terms of one or more of three main characteristics: the income of the borrower, their status as first time buyers, and the status of the property as new construction. Thus, where income limits are applied, access to low interest mortgage loans can be restricted to low or lower-middle income households; where it is restricted to new construction it can be expected to act as a direct incentive to new building; and where it is limited to first time buyers, it is directed at marginal households who are helped to overcome the heavy entry costs of owner occupation. The First Home Owners Scheme that was introduced in Australia in October 1983 and which is restricted to first time buyers whose incomes are less than 155 per cent of the national average provides an example of this type of targeting.

## FUTURE POLICY DIRECTIONS FOR ASSISTANCE TO OWNER OCCUPIERS

Among all OECD countries there is a strong commitment to improving housing standards and for many the expansion of owner occupation is seen as a major means of pursuing this objective. At the same time, governments are becoming acutely aware of the constraints on public expenditure and the limits these place on individual sectoral expenditure programmes. Within the housing sector this suggests that, in the future, greater attention will need to be paid to the design of cost effective policy instruments. This is especially true in the case of assistance to owner occupiers which, in many countries, is the largest and most rapidly growing item of expenditure. The systems in operation in individual Member countries and the assessment of them presented in the previous section, provide a basis for examining policy choices and suggesting some directions for improving the design of future policies.

First, an assessment of the economic case does not suggest that low interest loans are necessarily more efficient than tax expenditures (or vice versa) as a means of subsidising owner occupation; although it is usually possible to target direct assistance more effectively on a regional basis. In essence, though, both forms of subsidy effectively reduce the user cost of housing and thereby enable more to be consumed that would be the case in the absence of the subsidy. One possible complication associated with tax expenditures is that, because they influence effective income tax rates, they may have some marginal impact upon the supply of labour. However, in the absence of different interest and tax expenditure elasticities of demand, there is no reason to expect differences in public expenditure per additional unit of owner occupied housing consumed to result from use of the alternative instruments. Of more importance, as both are demand side subsidies (with the exception of cases where interest subsidies are given to developers), there is a need to ensure that the supply side of the industry can respond to additional demand. Otherwise, subsidies will be capitalised into house prices and merely be a source of capital gain rather than a source of additional housing.

As well as the relative economic impacts of interest rate subsidies and tax expenditures, attention also needs to be paid to their respective administrative arrangements. On the one hand, tax expenditure programmes do not require a separate bureaucracy for their administration as the tax authorities already have the machinery for monitoring and collecting tax revenues. Thus, there may be significant administrative cost savings through their use. These are likely to be most pronounced in countries with well developed tax systems having comprehensive coverage. Moreover, in terms of political feasibility, because tax expenditures are not usually subject to regular review and scrutiny, they may be viewed as a more stable means of subsidising housing than low interest loans which are more "visible." Certainly property owners can usually rely on tax-assistance and therefore include it in their long term plans. On the other hand, the more covert nature of tax expenditures may act against attempts to control costs. Moreover, in some countries there are differences of opinion between spending Departments and the Treasury. There is sometimes a reluctance to place housing subsidy instruments under direct Treasury control, as they are when administered through the tax system, and a preference for keeping them within the Department with a direct responsibility for housing, as is usually the case with interest rate subsidies.

To summarise, there are relative advantages and disadvantages associated with the use of low interest loans and tax expenditures that individual countries will need to consider. But these do not suggest a decisive case in favour of one or the other. Optimal choices will depend on individual national circumstances and preferences. However, it is the way in which the programmes are structured -- whether interest subsidies or tax expenditures -- that requires far more attention. It is to this issue that we now turn.

The main conclusion to emerge from this study of owner occupiers is that public expenditure on subsidies should be far more selective and carefully targeted in terms of its underlying objectives. This judgement applies equally to low interest loan schemes and tax expenditure programmes; however, it is of particular relevance in the latter case because, at the moment, the majority of tax expenditure programmes exhibit far too little selectivity. In many countries, a large proportion of total expenditure is directed towards relatively affluent, long standing owner occupiers living in good quality housing. In the future there is a strong case for targeting scarce public funds in terms of one or more of the following categories:

-- Households on low incomes;

-- Households wishing to enter or having recently entered the housing market such as first-time buyers;

-- Households with special needs, e.g. people with handicaps, mental disabilities etc.;

-- Household expenditure on specific aspects of housing for which the social benefit is greater than the private benefit, e.g. energy saving features;

-- Households moving into or improving dwellings in areas undergoing revitalisation where the social benefit is greater than the private benefit.

## A. Low Income Households

One of the main aims of subsidisation should be to assist those households who have insufficient purchasing power to acquire satisfactory housing in their own right. Within the owner occupier sector, the number of households within this category can be expected to increase in the future as the extent of ownership spreads and increasingly marginal households enter the sector. Consequently, tax expenditures should be targeted far more closely on these households. Restrictions on the amount of tax expenditure per household and the maximum tax rate at which allowances are offered represent possible ways of limiting subsidy: income ratios. But these devices are fairly coarse. In principle, a tax expenditure system in which there is a continuous income related taper would be preferable. In addition, there is a case for offering assistance through tax credits, which are payable to non tax paying as well as tax paying households, instead of tax allowances or exemptions.

In devising income related, tax expenditure schemes at least two complicating factors need to be taken into account. First, there is the problem posed by variations in household income over the life cycle. Housing is a good that is consumed over the entire life cycle and ability to pay will therefore be affected by variations in income over time. Devising a system in which the level of subsidy varies with variations in current income could be administratively complicated and would, in any case, take insufficient account of the long term nature of the consumption process. One approach to this problem which is worth considering is some form of fixed lifetime tax credit. Even here, though, some mechanism would be necessary for coping with households with insufficient foresight or those adversely affected by genuinely unforseen events.

The second problem associated with income related subsidisation is that it may accentuate the poverty trap in those countries where there is already a range of non-housing, income related benefits. This will be an issue for individual governments to resolve in the light of their particular range of subsidy schemes.

## B. New Entrants to Owner Occupation

For most households there are considerable financial barriers to entry to owner occupation. First, there are various transaction costs associated with the transfer of property which must be met. Second, there is usually a requirement that the household provides a proportion of the purchase price from their own resources. Savings accumulated over time are the usual source of such capital downpayments. Third, the real value of interest and capital repayments tends to be higher at the start of the mortgage loan period. This is the well known problem of front loading. Finally, most households enter owner occupation at an early stage in their careers when their incomes are modest.

If the aim of policy is to assist households to overcome these barriers, there is a strong case for targeting subsidies more towards households who are on the margins of owner occupation. In practice this would mean restricting subsidisation to the periods immediately prior and post entry to the sector. Numerous programmes which have these characteristics are in operation already in a number of OECD countries, but there is an argument for expanding them at the expense of general subsidisation. Examples of programmes which contain the necessary features are: the preferential tax treatment of savings schemes through which households accumulate down payments; the sales and transfer tax exemptions and/or allowances offered to first time buyers; and low interest loans or tax concessions offered over a specified number of years of the first mortgage.

Subsidy programmes which are targeted at marginal owner occupiers are based upon a recognition that the majority of households can expect their financial circumstances to improve considerably over their working lifetimes. For them, low income and difficulty of access to owner occupation is a temporary phenomenon. Consequently, no assistance would be offered to established owners beyond this period, or when they engage in subsequent transactions.

## C. Specific Housing Characteristics

In those countries where the basic housing needs of the majority of the population have been met, attention is increasingly turning towards methods of improving the quality of the housing stock. The targeting of housing subsidies to owner occupiers could play a far greater role in this policy than it has, in most cases, done to date.

The basic rationale for assisting home owners with the costs of improving the value of their private property is that the social return which the country expects to result from the investment is greater than the private return expected by the home owner. This may be because the time horizon over which individual take decisions is shorter than that which the government takes into account; or that individuals neglect certain factors (e.g. the

53

strategic consequences of being dependent on certain goods which need to be imported) that the government must consider. In any event, without a subsidy which reflects the divergence between the private and the social rate of return, such cases will result in an underinvestment in the desirable housing characteristics.

Some countries already operate subsidy policies of this type. Schemes to encourage investment in energy saving devices represent one example. There are also subsidy programmes designed to ensure certain minimum design and space standards in newly built property. There is, however, scope for redirecting general subsidisation of owner occupation towards specific reinvestment expenditures on a far wider scale. In devising such programmes, though, governments should take care to distinguish between reinvestment expenditure that results primarily in private benefits which are recouped by the owner himself, and those which generate substantial external benefits. In the former case, subsidies may still be appropriate, but there is a case for making them income related. In the latter case, this may not be desirable if the subsidies are part of a general urban revitalisation strategy.

## D. Urban Reinvestment

Urban revitalisation programmes represent areas where far greater emphasis on targeting reinvestment expenditures is particularly necessary. This subject is dealt with more fully in Chapter VI, but in the context of the subsidisation of owner occupiers, governments should consider the extent to which the relative subsidisation of acquisition costs at the expense of occupancy costs has contributed to a deterioration in the quality of the housing stock and suburban sprawl. Both of these problems would be reduced by greater attention to targeting on reinvestment in the inner city.

## E. Conclusions

It is important to stress that the preceding proposals for changes in the subsidy treatment of owner occupiers should not take place in isolation. There are obviously important linkages between the owner and rental sectors. Indeed, the proposals for greater targeting are one element in a general recommendation for greater tenure neutrality in housing subsidisation. The other elements in the approach are described in the remaining chapters of the report.

It is also important to point out that, in recommending such an approach, the issue of political and administrative feasibility will be of crucial importance. One of the main obstacles to the introduction of more rational systems of housing finance will be the vested interest of those groups of households who would be adversely affected. In the case of the withdrawal or reduction of tax expenditures from some groups, this opposition may well derive from very real fears of capital losses resulting from downward capitalisation. That is, falls in property prices resulting from the reduced purchasing power of non targeted households or properties. To avoid these problems careful thought will need to be given to the design of transitional arrangements. These might involve the phased withdrawal of subsidies over a number of years; or the compensation of existing owners in the form of some kind of capital sum which would be related to the discounted value of the future tax concessions that would be withdrawn.

In conclusion, it should be emphasised that the spread of owner occupation in practically all OECD countries has been a major source of the improvement of housing standards. In the majority of cases, it has succeeded in combining the individual household's quest for self improvement with the production of a socially desirable outcome. And government subsidies to owner occupiers have assisted this process. However, there have been a number of adverse consequences. Moreover, in the current climate of concern about levels of public expenditure, the growth in the cost of general subsidisation appears excessive. Subsidy arrangements that sufficed in periods when public expenditure constraints were less binding are now looking increasingly obsolete. This is the context in which greater attention to targeting is recommended.

Chapter IV

## HOUSING LOAN FINANCE

In Chapter III various subsidy schemes for assisting owner occupiers were discussed. All of these are designed to enhance households' ability to pay for this type of housing. However, for ability to pay to be translated into effective demand, it is necessary for debt finance to be available. This is because average house prices are typically three or more times average annual household income. Moreover, the size of a mortgage loan in relation to annual income means that house purchase is uniquely dependent on long term consumer credit. In most countries, specialist lending institutions and financing instruments have grown up in order to provide this credit. During the 70s these institution and their lending practices were subjected to some severe strains. Notable among these were pressures resulting from:

-- Inflation;

-- Interest rate volatility;   and

-- Fluctuations in the supply of funds.

In response to these pressures, a number of countries devised innovative financial instruments. Others introduced even more fundamental policy changes. Both, however, had the aim of increasing the household's ability to afford owner occupier housing and maintaining its supply. In this chapter, these changes   -- and their relevance for the 80s and beyond -- are examined in the context of the problems which originally gave rise to them.

## A. Inflation

Inflation exerts an adverse effect on housing loan-financing arrangements in two main ways. First, inflation tends to be incorporated into loan contracts through higher rates of nominal interest on borrowed funds. And since interest charges are a major proportion of the total annual cost of housing, these increases result in substantial increases in housing payments for those households dependent on loan finance. Second, inflation worsens the problem of "front end loading": that is, the tendency for the burden of the mortgage payments -- expressed as a proportion of household income -- to be higher in the early years of a loan.

Front end loading arises because, with a conventional housing loan of the type found in most OECD countries, the borrower repays the principal and meets the interest charges via a series of repayments that are fixed in nominal terms over the period of the loan. Even in period when there is zero inflation, but growth in real incomes, this arrangement will mean that mortgage repayments will fall as a proportion of income through time. However, with inflation, this effect is exacerbated because:

-- Increased interest rates will lead to an immediate rise in monthly repayments; and

-- The rate of growth of nominal earnings is likely to be boosted by inflation above the previous rate of growth of real earnings.

When, as is usual, the amount of loan principal exceeds annual household income by a substantial amount, there will be a larger absolute increase in initial monthly mortgage payments (through increased rates of interest) than in monthly incomes (through more rapid growth in earnings). Subsequently, the repayments-income ratio will decay more rapidly through time. Thus the higher the rate of inflation, the more the repayments profile is "tilted" towards the earlier years of the loan.

The consequences of the interaction of inflation and front end loading impact particularly strongly on first time buyers, both through an increase in the initial repayments burden and a widening of the "deposit gap". The latter phenomenon refers to the difference between the maximum loan that a household can secure and the property purchase price -- a difference that is usually financed by household savings. Because the maximum loan tends to be determined by the ability of the household to finance repayments from current income, and the size of a loan associated with a given level of repayments falls with inflation and rising interest rates, so the deposit gap increases with inflation.

The increase in initial repayments resulting from inflation does, of course, have its counterpart in house price appreciation. As this can be expected to rise along with general price inflation, while the size of the mortgage loan is fixed in nominal terms, the household's equity share in the property will rise. In effect, this represents real saving. However, it is likely that the first time buyer who is struggling to meet the initial repayments burden is being forced to undertake a rate of saving in excess of the rate he would freely choose.

In short, the conventional annuity mortgage, in an inflationary environment, places an excessive share of the repayments burden on the early years of a loan and may, thereby, deter entry into owner occupation. As a response to this problem, a number of financing initiatives aimed at re-shaping the time profile of repayments have been devised.

One example used in some countries is a system of deferred payment mortgages. These offer the borrower greater flexibility by allowing annual repayments to increase over time as ability to repay the loan (i.e. income) also increases. In the early years of the loan, repayments may not cover the interest charges with the result that the size of the principal increases. But, in time, repayments may be expected to "catch up" so that the principal starts being repaid.

The main aim of deferred mortgage arrangements is to bring into owner occupation those marginal households that would otherwise be unable to buy.

The system has the effect of providing the borrower with more money for house purchase than under a conventional annuity loan, and it take account of the future time profile of household income. The main risk on the borrower's side is that the commitment to higher payments in the future may lead to difficulty if interest rates rise sharply during the duration of the loan (see discussion of adjustable rate mortgages below). From the lender's point of view this is also a problem if the rising amount of principal is unsecured.

A more specific method of spreading the burden of repayment more evenly across the loan period is embodied in a system of index linked mortgages. Under this arrangement, the rate of interest payable on a loan is set at the real rate (i.e. not adjusted in response to inflation), while the principal sum is adjusted in line with inflation so that additional payments are spread over the entire mortgage term. Of course, if inflation continues over a number of years, the cash sum required for capital repayment increases each year; but, as with a deferred payment mortgage scheme, rising household incomes through time will usually enable the borrower to meet these payments. Once again, the capital sum which a borrower can safely afford is considerably larger with an indexed linked loan than with a conventional annuity mortgage.

Yet another means of reducing the impact of front end loading is offered by equity or shared appreciation mortgages. With this form of loan the borrower relinquishes part of his claim to future capital gain on the property, in return for lower initial payments. Thus the lender owns a share in the capital appreciation of the mortgaged property. Such schemes can be expected to be particularly popular with lenders in periods when substantial capital growth is expected. There are, however, certain technical problems concerning the formulation of equity mortgages. Most notably, a precise formula specifying the way in which the lender and borrower share in price apprecation has to be designed. Two main approaches are possible. On the one hand, the increase in the value of the individual property in terms of its original purchase price and eventual sale price may be used. In this case adjustments have to be made for price appreciation resulting from the owner occupier's own improvement expenditures. Alternatively, price appreciation may be based on the movements in a general price index, either relating to inflation generally or house price inflation. The use of a general index does, of course, involve the risk that the value of an individual property may not move in line with overall prices. If the individual property price rises by less than the general price, the owner occupier will be left with a smaller share of the capital gain and, possibly in some extreme cases, a debt obligation to the lender after the sale of the property.

Despite the widespread availability of mortgage instruments that enable the borrower to shift some of the repayment burden into the future (various schemes exist in, inter alia, Australia, Canada, France, Portugal, Turkey, United Kingdom and the United States), they are rarely used extensively -- even in times of rapid inflation. Explanations for low take-up rates range from the lack of publicity given to such schemes in some countries to claims about consumer caution in relation to new and unfamiliar financing arrangements. Sometimes, in contrast to the more usual claims about individuals' time preference and risk aversion, it is argued that individuals are willing to accept the current costs of front-end loading in return for expected gains from inflation in future years. There is also some evidence of caution on the part of the suppliers of loan finance. Some are unsure about rates of indexing and feel that it may not be sufficient to cover the increasing debt involved in deferred payment mortgages.

# B. Interest Rate Volatility

As well as experiencing historically high rates of price inflation during the 70s, many OECD countries also experienced unprecedentedly large variations in interest rates. For example, between 1970 and 1980, the range of dispersion in the real long-term rate in the major OECD countries covered in this report was: United States (-2.1 to +2.0); Japan (-9.4 to +5.9); France (-2.6 to +3.0); Germany (+0.2 to 4.4); United Kingdom (-9.7 to +3.6); and Canada (-5.7 to +3.7).

This volatility posed serious problems for those countries, such as Canada, the United States and the Netherlands, where mortgage loans were lent long-term at fixed rates of interest. In other countries, however, such as Australia, Germany and the United Kingdom, these problems were mitigated because of the longstanding existence of adjustable rate mortgages (ARMs). In the light of these experiences both the United States and Canada have, in recent years, adopted the ARM system (see below).

Basically, an ARM is a long term loan on which the rate of interest may be changed, usually at the discretion of the lender, during the term of the mortgage contract. It is a means of reconciling the borrower's and lender's interests in financial markets where institutions borrow short and lend long, and are susceptible to frequent interest rate changes. It is argued that not only do variable rates reduce cyclical fluctuations in the housing market, but that they have the merit of ensuring equity between borrowers because everyone is paying the same rate irrespective of the vintage of their loan. The major disadvantage of ARMs is that a borrower may be faced with an unexpected increase in mortgage payments. This is likely to be a particularly serious problem during the early years of a mortgage loan. To some extent, this problem may be reduced by the rearrangement of the time profile of repayments in the ways discussed above.

The experiences of those countries in which ARMs have been introduced relatively recently provide some good examples of the situations with which they are designed to cope. In the United States, for instance, specialist housing finance institutions -- the savings associations and savings banks -- are effectively forced to borrow short and lend long. This worked well during the 50s and 60s. Interest rates were stable and therefore there was little risk of the yield on mortgages lagging behind the cost of funds. Furthermore the rate of interest that could be obtained on long term loans was considerably higher than the cost of short term deposits, partly because of regulation Q, which held down rates artificially, and gave the savings associations a statutory interest rate advantage over the commercial banks.

As interest rates increased during the late 70s the problems inherent in such a system became more obvious. Since the banks and savings institutions were not permitted to offer market interest rates on deposits, money market mutual funds emerged: these were a device designed to allow the small investor to obtain market rates of interest. The growth of money market mutual funds was dramatic. In January, 1980 they held funds amounting to $55 bn. By July, 1981 the figure had increased to $142 bn. Gradually, the savings associations were allowed to compete by offering more attractive, market related terms. Hence, by the end of 1981, 70 per cent of savings balances were earning market related rates compared with only 10 per cent in 1978. Unfortunately, though, there was no accompanying liberalisation on lending rates. The institutions therefore saw the cost of funds rising rapidly, while being unable to alter their yields on existing loans. The result was that in 1981 the industry incurred a massive deficit.

The first response to this state of affairs was to allow the savings associations to diversify their activities in the hope that the profits earned on these activities would subsidise their mainstream business. However, the body of opinion in favour of more fundamental reform, through the adoption of ARMs, was growing. Then, in April 1981, the Federal Home Loan Bank Board -- which was the regulatory body for savings institutions -- authorised the introduction of ARMs.

By 1984, ARMs had become well established in the US market, accounting for nearly two thirds of loans. Most associations offer a lifetime limit on the extent to which rates can be increased, and many lenders also have an annual limit. The rates are, therefore, rather less adjustable than, say, the British equivalent.

The Canadian experience provides another example of changing market conditions that have led to the adoption of ARMs. At the end of the 70s, the Canadian housing finance system, with its five year mortgage roll-over, was highly regarded. It seemed to combine the best of both worlds. The institutions were able to borrow funds on a five year basis, and lend them out at rates that were fixed for five years. There is no doubt that this system did work effectively. However, as interest rates became more volatile, the deficiencies of the system became more apparent. The rate of interest that borrowers became committed to over a five year period depended not only on when they took out their loan, but also on when the five year renewal clause became operative. The volatile interest rates of the early 80s produced great inequities between borrowers, many of whom became reluctant to commit themselves for five year periods, and instead sought shorter term financing. The lending institutions reacted by offering loans with terms ranging from three years to one year and, exceptionally, six months., These enabled borrowers to speculate on interest rates. Clearly, though, as the term of a fixed interest loan is reduced so it approaches an ARM. Not surprisingly, therefore, variable rate loans have now become more widely available.

Trends in some other countries may also be noted briefly. In both the Netherlands and Japan, deposit taking banks have introduced variable rate loans. In Spain recent financial reforms, which have enabled the emergence of a mortgage bond market, represent the first attempt to introduce variable rate loans.

Clearly, the widespread adoption of ARMs suggests that they are a necessary form of loan finance instrument in those countries where lending institutions borrow short and lend long, and where interest rates fluctuate widely.

C. The Supply of Funds

Another more general aspect of interest rate policy during the 70s was the tendency for many governments to engage in regulation of the price and terms on which housing loan finance was offered. Usually, this meant insulating the market for housing finance in some way from other financial markets so that the mortgage interest rate could be set at a level below prevailing commercial rates. The major adverse consequence of this regulation was that there was a decrease in the flow of funds into housing, especially in periods of rising market interest rates. The extent of this problem varied considerably between countries depending on the size of interest rate differentials and the extent of subsidised, public sector lending. Those countries, such as the United States, which are predominantly reliant on private lending institutions, and which have also often operated fixed interest rate mortgages, have tended to fare worst. In addition, it has also sometimes been claimed that the rationing of finance caused by regulation places high risk borrowers on lower incomes at a particular disadvantage when non price methods of allocation are used. According to this view regulation not only restricts the availability of finance -- and is therefore inefficient -- but also has inequitable, income distributional consequences.

In response to these criticisms, a series of policy changes designed to improve the flow of funds into housing have been introduced in a number of countries. Among these, the most noticeable trend has been the deregulation of interest rates. This has taken place to a great or lesser extent in Australia, Canada, Finland, Greece, Japan, New Zealand, Sweden, United Kingdom and the United States. By allowing housing finance institutions to match the commercial market interest rates offered to depositors elsewhere, artificial restrictions on the flow of funds are removed.

At the same time as greater interest rate competitiveness has been introduced, attention in some countries has turned towards ways in which a greater volume of institutional investment funds may be attracted into the housing market. The scope for this depends, to a large extent, on the form of institutional lending structure presently operating in individual countries. At the moment, there are four main ways in which institutional funds are directed into the housing market.

The first way is via direct lending to house buyers. This method is used predominantly by banks, but also by some insurance companies. It is, however, increasingly unattractive for financial institutions, other than deposit taking institutions, to hold and service house purchase loans. This is because it is a labour intensive activity requiring an extensive branch network. For this reason, among others, insurance companies have been tending to take a declining share of the residential mortgage market. However, many insurance companies, pension funds and other financial intermediaries would like residential mortgages as part of their loan portfolios as they usually combine low risk with an acceptable level of profitability. One way of meeting this requirement, but avoiding the need of originating and servicing mortgage loans themselves, is to get mortgage lending institutions to make loans on their behalf. While it is unusual for specialist mortgage loan institutions to act on behalf of others, some banks operate in this way. For example, the Bank of Scotland has a number of "home loan syndicates"; the other members of the syndicates are foreign banks. The Bank of Scotland makes and services the loans, but they are financed equally by all the members of the syndicate.

A second way of attracting institutional funds into the housing market in times of mortgage shortages is via direct loans to housing finance institutions. This system is in use in many countries, particularly between linked institutions. For example, in France, the largest specialist lender, the Union de Crédit pour le Bâtiment (UCB), is part of the Compagnie Bancaire Group. The Compagnie Bancaire makes direct loans to UCB which, in turn, lends to house buyers. A similar arrangement exists between the Rabobank in the Netherlands and its subsidiary mortgage bank.

A third method is for institutions to purchase securities issued by housing finance institutions. For the institutional investor these represent a fairly liquid asset. This method is used in the United Kingdom where building societies issue bonds and certificates of deposit. Similarly, specialist mortgage lenders issue securities that are purchased by other financial institutions; in fact, there is a statutory obligation on the financial institutions to hold a certain quantity of securities. This secures the flow of funds into the housing market and permits the offer of housing loans at favourable rates of interest.

The fourth main way of channeling institutional funds is through secondary mortgage markets. These allow the housing finance institutions which originate and service mortgage assets to sell them to other institutions which hold them in their loan portfolios. Such arrangements have been of limited significance in most countries, but are of major importance in the United States. One of the main reasons for their popularity in the United States has been the existence of Federal regulations which require banking institutions to operate within their own state borders. There is, though, no guarantee that the demand for funds will match the supply of funds in a particular state. In fact, there has been a tendency for assets to have been concentrated in the established areas in the East, but for demand to be growing most rapidly in the Sunbelt states of the South and West. The secondary market orginally developed to enable lenders in the East to finance activity in the West.

There was a huge expansion of secondary mortgage markets in the United States during the early 80s. Their growth has been assisted by government agencies which underwrite mortgage debt. Thus mortgage assets have been effectively transformed into fixed rate government backed securities which have been attractive to institutional investors. From the original lending institutions point of view -- that is, the institution which continues to service the debt at fixed interest rates -- secondary mortage markets offer a way of increasing their lending activity and avoiding the interest rate risk posed by a system of fixed rate mortgages. However, with the growth of variable rate mortgages, the secondary mortgage market is becoming rather less important.

## D. Policy Issues for the Future

The deregulation of mortgage interest rates and the growth of various instruments attracting institutional investments into the housing market has meant that there is no longer a major problem of shortages in the supply of funds. Many housing finance markets are now more closely integrated with general finance markets and can compete for funds. In the face of fluctuations in the demand for and supply of funds the cost of credit now assumes some of the adjustment function, replacing the need to rely on non price rationing criteria.

From the borrower's point of view, these developments mean that the supply of mortgage credit will be increased in the future but also that the cost and the variability of this cost can be expected to increase. The medium term macro economic outlook (discussed in Chapter I) suggests that most countries can expect a modest rate of price inflation, but that real rates of interest are likely to remain high and volatile. The increasing integration of international capital markets suggests that interest rate volatility will grow as a problem as domestic interest rates within particular countries are affected by international financial flows. These developments pose a potential problems for marginal and first time owner occupiers. On a more optimistic note, however, the range of deferred payment, index linked and equity sharing mortgages, which were developed in response to the inflationary conditions of the 70s, also offer a means of coping with the short term problems associated with volatile interest rates. In those countries where the growth of owner occupation is dependent on the movement of households on modest incomes into the sector, these instruments have the potential to play a far larger part in mortgage arrangements than they have done to date.

## E. Housing Loan Finance for Urban Areas

Most of the issues surrounding housing loan finance concern the housing market generally, but some of them have specific urban implications. For example, the increased cost of funds may pose problems for young, newly formed households in those urban areas where regeneration strategies depend upon the ability to attract such households to previously run down locations. On the other hand, the greater competitiveness between lending institutions -- and their ability to charge rates of interest that reflect the risk on individual properties and borrowers -- should mean that more funds are available in areas in need of reinvestment than was the case under a more risk-averse, regulated system.

At a more aggregate level, a number of countries have recognised the need to attract private-sector, institutional funds to urban areas as part of their reinvestment strategies. Just as the shortage of funds, sometimes as a result of "redlining" and other discriminatory practices, contributed to the cumulative decline of these areas, so their regeneration will require private sector finance. This is likely to be particularly important in view of the tighter constraints on public expenditure which can be expected to continue into the medium term future. Ideally these funds will be needed to finance both owner occupation and the provision of rental housing. To facilitate their injection into the designated areas there are a range of urban development strategies that require more widespread implementation (see Chapter VI).

Chapter V

## POLICIES TOWARDS THE RENTAL SECTOR

Although there is a general emphasis on the expansion of owner occupation, most countries still have large stocks of rental housing. Indeed, in France, Germany, the Netherlands and Sweden the rental sectors are larger than the owner occupier sectors. Moreover, the rental sector tends to be particularly important in urban areas where, as a proportion of the housing stock, it is usually far larger than in rural areas. This is especially true of inner city areas.

Recent changes in the economic and social climate have meant that the rental sector has become the focus of renewed interest. These suggest that it will continue to play an important and, in some cases, growing role in the provision of housing. First, as far as economic factors are concerned, the economic recession -- with its slower rates of income growth and large scale unemployment -- has meant that substantial sections of the population will not have the purchasing power to contemplate entry into owner occupation. Even if the economic factors only serve to delay the stage in the life cycle when a family is in a position to enter the owner occupier sector, this will still result in a permanent increase in the stock demand for rental housing. Secondly, demand will be augmented by social and demographic factors leading to increasing numbers of elderly, single person households; greater numbers of young, single person households; additional households resulting from a higher incidence of marital breakdown; and single parent families. Although some of these households will gravitate towards the rental sector because of limited incomes and/or capital, for others renting will have characteristics that meet their preferences more closely than owner occupier housing. This will be the case, for example, for elderly households who wish to consume their capital during retirement, rather than having it tied up in housing, and for young, highly mobile households who are attracted by the lower transaction costs associated with movement in the rental sector.

These existing and future demands for rental housing will fall on three distinct types of housing supplier:

1. Private landlords who offer rental housing for profit.

2. Public (or social) housing agencies which typically build, own and manage stocks of housing which they let at subsidised rents.

3. Private, non-profit housing associations and co-operatives which are usually dependent on some form of government financial assistance.

This chapter considers each of these forms of ownership in turn. In doing so, it employs the common format of:

-- Describing the main policy instruments in operation in different countries;

-- Assessing the effectiveness of these policies in terms of their objectives; and

-- Putting forward proposals to improve the performance of each type of rental housing sector.


## THE PRIVATE, FOR-PROFIT, RENTAL SECTOR


The private rental sector was the Cinderella of housing policy during the expansionary period of the 60s and early 70s. Policy makers were more concerned to develop home ownership than encourage the building of new housing for renting, or to free the existing stock from the restrictions imposed on it in many countries during the immediate post-war period of housing shortages. This prolonged period of neglect has meant that the private rental market in many large conurbations is in a state of crisis. Recently, the long term decline of the sector has been exacerabated by cuts in real estate profits, at a time when new investment is being attracted to industrial investment by the higher returns it offers. The result has been the almost total disappearance of private investment in the rental sector in many countries.

What precisely has been the role of government in this process? And what are the prospects for improving the situation? In answer to the first question, it is possible to identify two main forms of policy instrument which have been employed towards the private rental sector in most countries. These are rent control and subsidies to private landlords.

## A. Rent Control

Rent control is a form of regulation which is designed to protect tenants from the high market rents which would otherwise result from shortages in the supply of rental housing. In most countries controls were initially introduced in response to short term shortages in rental housing, particularly during periods of war time, but they have tended to be retained long after the cessation of the initial cause. In the United Kingdom, for example, rent controls were first introduced during the First World War and, apart from a period between 1957 and 1964, have been in force in some form ever since. In the United States, they were also introduced in some cities as a result of shortages following the First World War. Subsequently controls have been in operation at different times in a number of cities and states. New York City has probably had the most widespread set of controls with an unbroken chain of legislation since the end of the Second World War. Australia has had waves of control, decontrol and recontrol operating at the State level. At present most of the traditional forms of control have disappeared but, as in the United Kingdom, they have been replaced by modified forms of rent regulation. In Sweden, controls were first introduced in 1942 and despite government commitments to abolish them during the 60s, they reappeared in a revised from during the 70s.

Although rent control policy takes a variety of specific forms in different countries, it usually comprises two components:

1. Specifying a maximum rent and/or rate of rent increase that a landlord can charge for a dwelling; and

2. Guaranteeing the tenant security of tenure at the designated rent as long as he fulfills his obligations.

Current legislation in many countries allows rents to be set with some regard to market levels, although there are usually specific restrictions. For example, a distinction is often made between the rent set on a new lease and the rate of increase on an existing lease. New rents are more likely to be set in line with representative rents found in the market. Thus in Germany, for example, when a new tenant moves in or a lease comes to an end, a new rent can be freely negotiated whereas, with existing lending agreements, rent increases must be in line with market rent increases. In France, rent is totally free on the first letting. When the lease is renewed, however, with or without a change of tenant, the rent is fixed with reference to the previous rent. The maximum permissable increase is decided by negotiation each year at the national level. However, the rent level cannot fall below a floor price stipulated by law (80 per cent of the reference index), and may be raised to the level of that on "similar" housing in cases where it is demonstrably lower. Rents under current leases are generally tied to a cost of living or building cost index. In addition, some countries set ceilings on the rate of rent increase as part of general anti-inflationary policy.

Practically all countries guarantee tentants security of tenure. Circumstances when a landlord is entitled to repossess his property are usually restricted to cases where the landlord or his family requires to live in the dwelling; where the tenant fails to fulfill his obligations in terms of rent payments, conditions of occupancy, etc.; or where major repair work on the property, or its demolition, is deemed necessary.

The regulation of rent levels and the terms of the transaction between the landlord and the tenant, represented by rent control, has been the subject of widespread criticism. Specifically, it has been claimed that it:

-- Deters investment in rental housing;

-- Leads to a misallocation of housing resources;

-- Is inequitable in its treatment of different groups of tenants;

-- Is inequitable in the treatment of landlords;

-- Involves excessive administrative cost.

Investment Disincentives

Rent control is held to deter investment in rental housing in a number of ways. First, by reducing the level of profits earned by landlords below the market rate of return, it acts as a direct disincentive to new investment. Even when newly constructed dwellings are explicitly exempt from controls, new construction is discouraged because it has to compete for tenants with existing buildings offering lower, controlled rents.

Furthermore, once the political climate for rent control is established, its extension to currently exempt properties becomes more likely. This uncertainty about the future form of policy is particularly important in the case of investment in a long lived asset such as housing.

Apart from the disincentive to new construction, rent control leads landlords to seek to reduce operating costs through the neglect of repair and maintenance expenditure. Hence the quality of private rented accommodation is subject to accelerated depreciation. In some cases, the decline of whole areas of rental housing within cities produces slum neighbourhoods which act as a deterrent to new investors. Consequently, housing may fall into the hands of unscrupulous slum landlords. In certain cities in the United States, for example, these landlords have abandoned buildings when they have been "milked" of all profitability and reached an exceptionally dilapidated state.

The stock of rental housing may be further depleted if the landlord has the opportunity to dispose of his asset in an unregulated market. This process has accounted for the disappearance of large quantities of rental housing in the United Kingdom as landlords have sold property into owner occupation when it becomes vacant.

### Misallocation

By holding rents below the market level, controls prevent the price system from providing signals which induce consumers to use the housing stock efficiently. Thus households composed of elderly individuals or couples often live in dwelling units far larger than their current needs require because they have no incentive to seek smaller accommodation. This makes it difficult for larger families to find housing. Moreover, these families are often dissuaded from searching for larger accommodation, if they are already in controlled property, because the marginal cost of an extra room in the decontrolled sector will be very high.

Misallocations in the housing market also often spillover into the labour market. If a tenant who quits controlled property is unable to find alternative housing at a rent similar to his previous controlled level, there is a disincentive for him to move. This reduces the mobility of labour and thereby reduces the capacity of the economy to adapt smoothly to industrial restructuring and other changes.

### Inequity Between Tenants

Controls tend to benefit tenants in a somewhat random manner. As a result, anomalies abound. Under most control systems, the greatest benefits are conferred on tenants who have occupied a dwelling for many years. Newly formed households, on the other hand, will often find difficulty in gaining access to the controlled sector. Similarly, newly arrived households -- who typically include a large number of minority groups -- also tend to find access to controlled housing difficult. As a result, newly formed and newly arrived households, both of whom tend to be on lower incomes than established households, are often required to pay higher, non-controlled rents. In short, controls tend to benefit existing tenants at the expense of future ones and, because tenants of controlled dwellings are not assessed in terms of their means, they often have perverse income distributional consequences.

## Inequity Towards Landlords

In most cases where the government decides that a particular group within the population merits some form of assistance, the government itself undertakes to bear the cost. It usually does this by paying the supplier so that he can sell the commodity below its full cost of production or by making a payment to the consumer, either in cash or in kind. In the case of rent control, however, government regulation protects the tenant but the cost of the implicit subsidy (i.e. the difference between the market rent and the controlled rent) is borne by the landlord. As well as having consequences for the supply and quality of rental housing, it is also argued that this is inequitable. Owners of rental property should not be called upon to bear the cost of a necessity: it should be borne by society at large through the government.

In addition, rent control may also be inequitable in the treatment of different types of owners. In many countries, it is the small scale landlord whose property is subject to rent controls. Often large scale property owners are more able to divert their investments into non-regulated parts of the property market.

## Excessive Administrative Costs

Controls are very expensive to administer. This is because they tend to grow in complexity and also because, if they are to be effective, they require close monitoring. There are powerful incentives encouraging evasion or illegal practices. Owners unable to charge market prices reflecting the scarcity of their assets often try to devise methods for collecting "under-the-counter" payments. Tenants faced by housing shortages and limited bargaining power are left with no alternative but to meet these payments. Even with large bureaucracies devoted to the regulation of rental markets, it usually proves impossible to stamp out completely these black market transactions.

Evidence in support of many of the criticisms listed above is found in numerous cities and countries in which rent controls have been imposed. Accounts from New York, San Francisco, Paris, London, Stockholm, Canberra and many other cities document serious shortages in the supply of rental housing and a lack of new private investment. Disinvestment is confirmed by condition surveys which indicate that the private rental sector contains a disproportionate amount of substandard housing. There are also numerous reports of rental property being converted into housing for owner occupation, condominium developments, etc. where there is no regulation on the sale price. Within the declining rental sector the coexistence of overcrowding and under occupancy suggests inefficiencies in the use of the existing stock.

However, it would be wrong to attribute all of these failings to the existence of rent control. The causes of the decline of the private rental sector are more complex than a simple correlation between rent control and the size/quality of the stock would suggest. To start with, if the specific impact of rent control is to be assessed, it is necessary to identify two distinct supply effects. On the one hand, it may be argued that investors are deterred from making new investments in rental housing because of the low returns it yields; on the other hand, there may be disinvestment in the existing stock, through depletions and/or qualitative decline.

As far as new investments are concerned, the exemption of new lettings from controls in the United Kingdom between 1954 and 1965 did little to revitalise investment. By way of explanation, it is sometimes argued that, because housing is an extremely durable asset, the investor will have a long time horizon, and the existence of rent control in one sector of the market will make him apprehensive about its extension to other areas in the future. While this interpretation of investor behaviour is plausible, there is nonetheless conflicting evidence. In France and some other European countries there was a private rental investment boom during the 60s and 70s despite the existence of various forms of rent control on existing properties. Economic conditions at the time were simply such that profitability appeared to be certain, and the prevailing optimism was sufficient to persuade people that there would be no great changes. Clearly there are other determinants of new investment in rental property besides rent control.

Some similar uncertainties surround the link between disinvestment and rent control. In the United Kingdom rent controls were abolished on existing dwellings becoming vacant over the period 1957 to 1965, but this did little to stem the tide of sales into owner occupation which took place at 2-4 per cent per year. Once again other factors seem to have been at work. What are these factors?

In addition to rent control, three factors have contributed to the present crisis in the private rental sector. Two of these affect the supply side of the market, and one, the demand side. First, on the supply side, the long term decline of private renting in many countries has been associated with the growth of alternative investment opportunities for small scale savers. Individuals who, in the past, would have been likely to invest in housing because of the security of the asset, now have access to a wider range of financial intermediaries offering comparable security but greater liquidity. The second supply side factor has been the relatively unfavourable tax treatment of rental housing investment in some countries (see below).

It could, of course, be conceded that both of these supply side factors have contributed to the decline of investment in rental housing but, at the same time, maintain that if rents had been allowed to rise they would have counteracted these adverse effects. However, this view presupposes that the demand for privately rented housing would have been sufficiently strong to sustain these rent increases. In fact, in many countries demand has been shifting away from the rental sector for reasons unconnected with rent control. In particular, there has been the growth in the demand for owner occupation resulting from rising incomes and/or favourable tax treatment. Furthermore, the expansion of social housing has reduced the demand for private renting from many low income families who would previously have been accommodated in the sector.

B. Subsidies to Private Landlords

Private rental housing receives both direct and indirect subsidies. Direct subsidies are available in a limited number of countries in the form of low interest loans (e.g. Canada, Japan, the United States). More generally, in most countries, the private rental sector receives preferential tax treatment in comparison with commercial or industrial investment. Thus, although income from rental property is, in principle, subject to personal income tax or corporation tax, depending on the status of the owner, it is usually subject to special conditions as far as the tax deductibility of costs and certain tax exemptions are concerned.

The main cost item on which preferential treatment is allowed is depreciation. In the majority of countries, depreciation can be set against gross rental income, though the methods of assessment vary quite widely. In France and the Netherlands, gross rental income is subject to a 15 per cent flat rate deduction for depreciation throughout the life of the property. This is a more generous rate than is applied to industrial and commercial assets. In the United States, the treatment of depreciation is a key source of investment financing. The rules in this area, which were already highly concessionary, were eased still further with the adoption of the Accelerated Cost Recovery System (ACRS) in 1981. The period of depreciation of housing investment is normally 20 years. For housing sold since 1st January 1981, taxpayers may opt either for linear depreciation or for accelerated cost recovery. In Germany, housing completed after 27 July 1981 is subject to a generous degressive depreciation rate of 5 per cent for the first 8 years, 2.5 per cent for the next 6 years, and 1.5 per cent for the ensuing 36 years. The United Kingdom is unusual in treating housing as an asset with an infinite life for tax purposes and allowing no deductions for depreciation.

Apart from depreciation costs, the tax systems in most countries allow private landlords to deduct general operating costs, such as maintenance and repair costs, insurance, management and loan charges, from gross income. Insofar as this is consistent with the general tax treatment of business income it does not represent a subsidy. However there are sometimes special circumstances in the case of housing taxation. In some countries (e.g. Canada, Germany, United States), if operating costs exceed gross income from the property, they may be set against the taxpayers total income. Other countries, however, limit the use of property deficits on the grounds that they encourage tax evasion. In France, for example, property deficits may only be set against property income for the first 5 years following acquisition.

Some countries allow specific tax deductions with the aim of encouraging investment in rental housing, particularly if this is directed towards the needs of low income households. In France, for example, private investment in the rental sector is encouraged by allowing the deduction from gross income of 5 per cent of the investment sum up to a specified ceiling.

A number of countries offer tax exemptions on income from certain types of rental housing. In the United States, for example, Real Estate Investment Trusts are taxed only on non-distributed profits, provided that at least 95 per cent of gross income is earned from real estate, and that at least 95 per cent of current income is distributed in the year of accrual or the following year. These terms are designed to increase the returns to equity holdings in the private rental sector and thereby enhance the attractiveness of this form of investment.

By directing financial incentives to the suppliers of rental housing, subsidies provide the potential for reducing the cost of rental housing to tenants without incurring the deleterious supply effects experienced with rent control. There is, however, some doubt about whether measures of this type have been sufficiently strong to overcome the adverse effects of rent control and deficiency of effective demand. Policy responses aimed at improving the performance of the private rental sector in the future will need to take account of all of the numerous factors which have combined to produce the existing unsatisfactory state of affairs found in so many countries.

## C. Future Directions for Policy

The basic need in the private rented sector is to ensure an adequate supply of housing at a price that households can afford. There are, therefore, two objectives: a supply objective and a price objective. Many of the problems associated with rent control have arisen because the supply objective has been neglected. Proposals for decontrol are designed to rectify this shortcoming. If rents are allowed to rise, it is argued, private investment funds will be attracted into the market. Certainly this has been the experience in Germany where a deregulated private market has flourished. Elsewhere, though, there is concern about the substantial time lags in the housing construction industry. Sudden decontrol may lead to large rent increases and considerable hardship to tenants as the supply of housing adjusts. Moreover, given the existence of large numbers of low income households within the sector, ability to pay at even long run equilibrium rents (i.e. the rent levels which would prevail after short run shortages had been eliminated) is only likely to be achieved if tenants receive some form of subsidy.

The preceding considerations suggest that policies aimed at revitalising the private rental sector should incorporate gradual decontrol with a system of housing allowances. In fact, housing allowances are already gaining popularity in a number of countries; especially as they are able to be targeted on low income or other households with specific characteristics. Thus in Australia they are offered to pensioners and are shortly to be extended to the unemployed. In Canada they are also offered to the elderly in some Provinces. Finland, Sweden, Denmark, Germany and Norway offer allowances on the basis of household income and family size. A similar system based upon rent levels and household income operates in the United Kingdom. In the Netherlands there is a government established norm rent which varies according to household income and allowances are paid if the actual rent is above the norm. There is also a rent adjustment scheme designed to stimulate mobility. Under this scheme, a proportion of any rent increase necessary to facilitate a change of location is eligible for subsidy.

In Germany about 10 per cent of all tenant households receive housing allowances (as do one per cent of owner occupiers). The amount of the allowance depends on the size of the household, the family income and their housing costs. Since housing allowances are geared to individual circumstances, they are a particularly accurate instrument. On average housing allowances cover about one-third of the housing costs of recipient households. About 45 per cent of all housing allowance recipients live in publicly assisted dwellings. Here housing allowances complement the use of public funds spent on subsidizing the property itself by providing an additional reduction of housing costs geared to each individual case. It is therefore not necessary to regulate publicly assisted rents in general. In the publicly assisted dwellings completed since 1970 about 20-25 per cent of the tenant households receive housing allowances.

The United States is notable for the extent to which reliance is being shifted to housing allowances or vouchers at the expense of other forms of housing subsidy. It is argued that they are more efficient than, say, public housing, because they require less government involvement and make maximum use of private market initiatives. They are also more easily targeted than many alternative subsidy programmes.

Of course, the pace of decontrol will need to take account of the existing demand and supply situation in individual urban areas. Where there are chronic shortages, there is always the danger that the introduction or expansion of housing allowances will simply fuel rising rent levels in the existing stock. These may persist for long periods of time if new investment is slow to materialise. Clearly considerable attention will need to be given to the actual mechanics of decontrol.

On the question of the actual method of decontrol, one proposal to emerge from the discussions of the Project Group would involve landlords paying a specified amount into a government controlled and administered fund when a controlled tenancy is terminated. In return, the property would be freed from rent control. The actual amounts to be charged for freedom from control could be based upon the discounted value of the difference between future controlled and uncontrolled levels. These would vary according to the "tightness" of particular local markets. In any event, the sums accumulated in the government fund would be available for funding housing allowances to tenants in particular need.

## PUBLIC SECTOR RENTAL HOUSING

In many countries public housing (1) has grown up in response to the need to control rents and ensure an adequate supply of good quality housing. Often this has been deemed necessary because of the failure of the private rental market to provide satisfactory accommodation at rent levels that households can afford. Among OECD countries, Sweden, the Netherlands and the United Kingdom have the largest stocks of public housing (see Table 11) although, in the case of the United Kingdom, between 15 and 20 per cent of the stock has been sold for owner occupation since 1980.

Current policy concerns involving public housing centre on four main issues:

1. The decline of large, often high-rise, estates;

2. The residualisation and social segregation associated with this decline;

3. The management of public housing;

4. Rent setting procedures.

### A. The Decline of Large Estates

Large high-rise estates played a considerable part in resolving post war housing shortages in a number of European countries. The widespread destruction of housing during the war, the cessation of building, the neglect of maintenance and repair work, urban migration and the post war baby boom all led to substantial excess demand. As governments had been directly involved in the mobilisation of resources during the war, public sector building was seen as a logical, direct response to this need. In France, for example, over the period of 1949-75, urban flats constituted almost one quarter of total new construction, so that now there are approximately 1 1/2 million units in high rise estates.

For those households who first came to live in them, flats on large housing estates constituted a marked improvement on the cramped conditions and decrepit state of their former homes. In many countries, acquiring accommodation on a new estate was considered to be a step up the ladder. Furthermore, large urban estates seemed to avoid the disadvantages of suburban sprawl.

Over the last 20 years, though, this earlier optimism has been replaced by widespread disillusion. Many serious defects in the design and functioning of large estates have become apparent. Community services have often been slow to develop. There has frequently been a considerable time lag between the arrival of residents and the provision of infrastructure and services. There has been a failure to undertake landscaping and other environmental services on a human scale. Basic design failings in the buildings themselves (e.g. inadequate insulation, faulty heating systems, condensation and dampness) and a cumulative neglect of repair and maintenance expenditure have combined to produce serious problems of housing decay. Moreover, these problems of physical deterioration have been associated with the social and economic decline of many of the affected areas.

## B. Social Segregation and Residualisation

A large proportion of problem estates are located in areas of high unemployment. These estates, notably in traditional industrial regions such as those found in France and the United Kingdom, are suffering from the same economic problems as the regions in general: widespread unemployment, large numbers of young jobless, increasing poverty and dependence on social security or other welfare payments. However, the density and concentration of these problems on the estates adds to their starkness. Elsewhere, estates are situated within or on the periphery of conurbations where, although their industries are not in such an acute state of recession as those in traditional manufacturing areas, they are none the less experiencing industrial restructuring. As the industrial fabric changes so does the composition of the housing estates. More affluent workers in the technology based industries move out and are replaced by those on low incomes including the unemployed, the elderly and single parent families. Often the unpopularity of housing in these areas means that much of it is difficult to let and, as a result, vacancy rates are high. Also in France, the Netherlands and the United Kingdom certain estates have disproportionately large numbers of ethnic minority groups who have arrived from former colonies and overseas territories over the last 20 years. Sometimes the housing which is available may not be entirely appropriate to their family sizes or cultural requirements.

In many ways public housing estates are being excluded from the mainstream economic life of the nation. They have become economically, socially and spatially segregated. In their insularity social problems abound. Destabilisation of the social structure gives rise to, inter alia, inter generational and inter racial tensions. There are also often high rates of vandalism and crime, especially drug related offences, and school absenteeism. In their most acute form, these areas have also been the scenes of urban riots such as those experienced in the United Kingdom in recent years.

But the situation in public housing, even on large scale estates, is not all gloom and despondency. In Sweden, the Netherlands, Germany and even in France and the United Kingdom -- where some of the worst problems exist -- there are large numbers of residents who are content with their housing and environment. And where they are not, a number of positive steps that recognise both the social and physical problems of the worst estates are being taken in response to tenants' preferences. Sensitive planning and design can obviously produce better housing conditions. In fact, in Japan one of the major objectives of social housing is the overall improvement of housing standards. Turkey places a similar reliance on public housing as a means of improving housing standards. And in Canada some of the problems of social segregation are addressed by limiting the proportions of particular income groups in Public Housing Association buildings.

## C. The Management of Public Housing

Many of the failings of public housing described above have been the focus of comprehensive rehabilitation strategies which have been introduced in a number of countries in recent years. These strategies operate on a number of different fronts. At the most obvious level, there are reinvestment strategies designed to improve the physical quality of the housing stock and its immediate environment. These strategies are discussed in Chapter VI as a part of the general consideration of reinvestment policies. In this chapter the discussion is limited to new initiatives in the organisation and management of public housing.

In numerous OECD countries there is widespread dissatisfaction with many of the old-style forms of centralised government activity. There is a strong feeling that centralised bureaucracies are insufficiently responsive to consumer or user needs. Accordingly, attempts are being made to devise new systems of organisation and management that are more accountable to users. This trend has already begun in the housing sector where the management of public housing has often been criticised for being excessively bureaucratic and centralised. To overcome these deficiencies, new initiatives aimed at the decentralisation of management functions to Local Authorities and the active encouragement of resident participation in the formulation and implementation of policy have been introduced in a number of countries. Elsewhere, sales of blocks of housing to social agencies or private management companies have sought to achieve similar aims.

Within these initiatives, tenant participation is considered to be particularly important. Too often the difficulties encountered on large estates are reflected in resident passiveness and a tendency for inhabitants to turn to welfare agencies in the event of problems rather than getting together to tackle them themselves. Although this lack of self-help is understandable with large numbers of poor and deprived families living in the areas, organisers and experts are agreed that it is a basic requirement for the sucessful regeneration of an area that tenants should participate not only in rehabilitation measures but also more generally in the longer term routine management of the areas.

Tenant Associations have been established for some years in the Nordic countries. Through their Associations, tenants not only play an active role in the formulation of rehabilitation strategies, allocation procedures etc., but they also participate in more general district activities such as running amenities, organising cultural events and so on. The aim is to make residents feel that they belong to a community and to give them a stake in its general improvement. In other countries such schemes are still in their infancy. However, since 1981, this approach has been adopted by the "Commission nationale pour le développement social des quartiers" in France. By 1986 the Commission covered 120 large development schemes. A similar approach was also adopted by the Priority Estates Project in the United Kingdom which covered 90 housing estates considered to be in need of priority treatment.

Of course, the decentralised control and tenant participation are not without their problems. Views about the most desirable policy for an area are bound to vary. Disagreements raise the question of representativeness: who represents whom? What mechanisms for resolving disputes should be used? In heterogeneous areas participatory planning can be a lengthy process. Moreover, the sources of funding for the majority of schemes will emanate from higher levels of government with their wider revenue raising capacities. This may well be a potential source of conflict if community preferences are viewed as undesirable by the funding bodies.

One aspect of problem estates which calls for particular attention through management initiatives is the growing incidence of social imbalance. As has already been described, poor and deprived families find themselves locked into areas which are shunned by households with any degree of choice. Housing officers are then faced with a short term dilemma; either they attempt to encourage greater social mix by refusing to allocate all accommodation to deprived households -- in which case housing will remain empty and susceptible to vandalism, etc. -- or they fill vacancies whatever the status of the applicant. In the latter case, the incidence of social imbalance will increase. In the short term it is very difficult to resolve this dilemma. Most commentators agree that it can only be satisfactorily resolved through medium term social restructuring; that is, social diversification must be approached on a city wide basis. This means widening the range of locations at which accommodation is made available for households presently concentrated on problem estates.

There is also a need for the reappraisal of traditional allocation procedures. More attention needs to be paid to the special needs of particular groups of households (e.g. handicapped persons, single parent families, elderly households, ethnic minority households, etc.). Among these groups needs will differ in terms of waking and sleeping hours, attitudes to children and tolerance of noise. In many cities best practices already pay attention to these types of factors, but there are still many estates where inter group frictions could be relieved by greater attention to these principles.

Within the United Kingdom, one of the government's responses to the decline of large areas of public housing has been to engage in a large scale programme of privatisation. This has involved the sale of public housing to tenants at substantial discounts on the market price and schemes which transfer the ownership of blocks of housing to private property companies, housing associations and tenant cooperatives. By 1986 nearly 20 per cent of the 1979 stock of public housing had been privatised in this way. It is evidently a very popular policy amongst those who are buying their own dwellings. Surveys have shown that the majority of public sector tenants would wish to become owner occupiers at some time in the future. And the effects on the ground can be marked, improving the visual image of at least parts of an estate, improving the confidence of those living on an estate and increasing their demands for better Council services. In addition the policy has increased the social mix within the public housing sector.

On the other hand the policy has not been without some criticism. Some commentators have argued that reducing the size of the stock of public sector housing, and removing the better quality dwellings from it have increased social and tenure polarisation.

At a more basic level it is generally recognised that, while housing policies such as those involving the devolution of management functions, can play a major part in the revitalisation of run-down areas of public housing, the malaise affecting these areas generally goes beyond the housing sector itself. The poor state of the housing is often a direct result of the poverty of the tenants. As such, regeneration strategies must also be concerned with local economic development. This is likely to be most effective if it is undertaken with the particular needs of these areas in mind. In this connection, schemes that create jobs locally have been developed with some success in a number of countries. These tend to use existing facilities to start shops, restaurants, small repair businesses, and private and public services. Often participatory or cooperative organisational structures are encouraged as an adjunct to the "community" approach that is adopted in relation to the area's housing itself. Considerable local effort often goes into the development of enterprise of this sort. Nonetheless where public funds are used for "seedcorn" purposes, each proposal should be assessed carefully in terms of its long term commercial viability. Experience suggests that local zeal can sometimes outstrip rational commercial judgements.

Finally it should be pointed out that management problems associated with size are not solely associated with public sector housing. Nor is the solution always found through internally generated re-organisation. In Germany, for example, publicly assisted housing enterprises have responded to competition from the free market. Responsibilities have been handed over to the employees of the enterprises who can take better and swifter account of the wishes of tenants. Formal tenant participation, on the other hand, does not play a significant role. However, it is felt that this experience shows the positive effect of free market competition. The pricing of publicly assisted dwellings is also partly influenced by competition. Rents have been lowered particularly in large housing estates and as a result the stock of vacant dwellings has been reduced.

## D. Public Housing Rents

Whatever measures are adopted to improve the fabric and management of public sector housing, there will be a need to develop more rational rent setting procedures. Not only will tighter restraints on overall public expenditure in the future lead policy makers in this direction, but the performance of the sector itself in terms of efficiency and equity will depend on the way in which rents are set.

At the moment many countries set rents at levels which cover historic costs but are below the level necessary to cover the economic costs of the housing. With inflation and fluctuations in interest rates, this way of setting rents tends to be inequitable. Households who obtained public housing at early dates are likely to pay lower rents than recent entrants to the sector, even though the recent entrants are probably more needy. Even when public authorities pool their historic costs and set rents in a way that covers these pooled costs, rents are rarely varied in a way that reflects the size and quality of different dwellings or the income level of the occupants. Thus the cost of housing of a given size and quality is likely to vary among households in ways unrelated to their needs.

Many rent setting methods also result in inefficiency. This is because they provide little incentive to use the stock of housing in an efficient manner. Allocation is largely based on administrative criteria and often attaches insufficient importance to consumer preferences. The absence of a pricing system which reflects the true costs of production and consumer preferences means that there is no good guide to what type of housing to build and where to build it. These shortcomings in the allocation process are more important in situations where large absolute shortages in housing have been overcome. In such cases it is no longer just a matter of providing a dwelling in which to live; housing provision needs to be more attuned to who wants what and where.

Another aspect of inefficiency arises because, with rents set below market levels, entry into public housing has to be rationed. Moreover, tenants are unable to obtain the precise amount of housing they would like at the administered rent. The rent and the dwelling constitute a tied offer. In welfare economics terms, this represents a source of "deadweight" welfare loss because the value of the subsidy to the tenant is likely to be less than its cost to the government.

Since household choice is over-ridden by limitations on entry into public housing and by constraints on the consumption of housing within the sector, there is almost certainly a misallocation of public housing among households. Furthermore, this misallocation may extend beyond the public housing sector. The supply of public housing and its administered rent levels affect market rents, house prices and eventually the supply of housing outside the public sector. For example, an increase in the supply of public housing could be expected to lower private sector rents and house prices in the short run, and the supply of other housing in the longer run. Conversely, a rise in public sector rents would shorten the queues for public housing and raise private sector rents and prices in the short run, and increase supply in the long term. This interdependence of housing sectors places an additional onus on governments to devise rational public sector rent and subsidy policies.

Of course, not all governments share the view that the private market should be used as a benchmark in terms of which the performance of public housing should be judged. The collective approach to provision and finance has a long established tradition in, for example, Sweden and the Netherlands and commands widespread support. Elsewhere, though, there is a growing trend towards charging rents which reflect market conditions coupled with income related subsidies or housing allowances for those households which need them. Australia, Canada, Germany, Japan, Luxembourg and the United Kingdom are among the countries which have moved in this direction in recent years. Such policies recognise that, once acute housing shortages have been overcome, the major rationale for subsidising public housing is on income distributional grounds. Given this aim, income related subsidies represent a more closely targeted policy instrument than across-the-board rent subsidies.

There is, however, one possible conflict between objectives on public housing that policy makers must bear in mind. This arises because targeting allowances on an income related basis may be expected to hasten the departure of higher income households from public housing, as they are not eligible for assistance, and to increase the inflow of lower income groups. While this represents an efficient use of public funds it can nonetheless lead to a reduction in social mix on public housing estates with the adverse consequences of segregation and residualisation described above.

In this context, it is worth considering the housing allowance approach adopted in the United States. One of the advantages claimed for this approach is that it avoids the social segregation of lower income groups that often occurs in public housing. In this approach, the belief that the private market operates more efficiently has led to a shift away from public sector provision. Instead, under "Section 8 Assistance" designated households receive subsidies towards the cost of private rented accommodation -- the amount depending on the household's composition and income level. To qualify, the household must have an income below a specified level and be willing to pay a given percentage of that income in rent. The government contracts to pay the difference between the rent charged by the landlord and the tenants' contribution. The actual rent charged is negotiated between the landlord and the government. Landlords who wish to participate in the scheme must come forward and tenants are directed to them by the government.

In comparison with the assistance offered to low income groups through public housing, it is claimed that this approach gives households greater freedom of choice over where to live, encourages the dispersal of low income households, and tailors the subsidy to the needs of the individual family. There is, however, a constraint on housing consumption similar to that found in public housing; namely, that in order to receive a subsidy a household must live in one of number of designated dwellings and the amount of the subsidy is tied to the one they choose. This constraint reduces the value of the subsidy to the tenant and is also the source of a "deadweight" loss. In addition, an extra dollar of rent in this type of subsidy system can cost the household nothing. Thus it can lead to inefficient use of the housing stock. In addition, assisted tenants have no incentive to bargain for cheaper rents and, at least in the American context, public authorities have proved to be poor bargainers.

This final consideration was an important source of concern surrounding the introduction of housing assistance. Specifically, it was feared that assistance would cause substantial increases in rents because of the sluggish supply response. This would mean that the subsidies found their way into landlords' pockets rather than benefiting low income tenants. In view of these concerns a number of housing allowance experiments were carried out. These suggested that fears of large price rises and little increases in supply were not warranted. Three main supply responses prevented large price rises. First, and most importantly, there was extensive upgrading of sub-standard property which was made possible by the low average cost of repairs and improvement. Second, since it took time for the impact of the programme on housing demand to accumulate, there was time for supply to adjust to the eventual extra demand. Third, there was a reduction in the vacancy rate.

Another important reason why there were not large price increases following the introduction of housing allowances in these U.S. experiments was that only about 40 per cent of eligible households chose to participate in them, probably because of the minimum standard requirement (i.e. only dwellings satisfying a given minimum standard were eligible for subsidy). Many low income families appear to have found that the minimum standard set by the government forced them to devote a larger portion of their income to housing than they would normally choose to do, and that housing assistance was insufficient to offset this higher expenditure. Furthermore, those households which did qualify for the housing allowance did not increase their housing expenditures by very much. In fact, those recipients already living in acceptable housing did not increase their standards at all. Thus, most recipients stayed in their present housing, making minor repairs when they were required in order to meet programme standards, and used most of the housing assistance to free their own funds for expenditure on other goods and services. Households which needed to increase their housing expenditure substantially in order to achieve the minimum standard, often involving a change of house, generally did not participate in the programme.

The American experience of housing allowance schemes suggests it may fail to make a significant improvement in housing standards although it would assist some low income households in paying for decent housing.

## E. Future Directions for Policy

To summarise, there are two main aspects of policy towards the public rental sector which need to be developed further: management and pricing. (A third aspect dealing with reinvestment strategies is discussed in Chapter VI.)

In response to criticisms of over centralised and bureaucratic administrative arrangements, a number of countries have been developing management systems which involve the decentralisation of functions and greater attention to tenants' views. These initiatives are in line with the growth of consumerism and greater producer accountability and offer scope for improved satisfaction with public housing.

On the question of pricing, there has been a movement away from rent schemes which offer across-the-board subsidies to all tenants, in favour of those which offer assistance in terms of the individual tenant's circumstances and income. These schemes permit more efficient targeting of subsidies onto lower income groups, but by influencing the socio-economic composition of the sector, they sometimes produce social imbalance and associated adverse consequences. This is an example of a conflict between two policy objectives. One solution that is being followed in some countries is the provision of public housing in small scale developments at locations throughout the city. This offers the scope for the integration of public housing tenants into the life of the city in a way that spatial segregation does not permit.

Apart from public housing which is directly owned and managed by government, many countries encourage the provision of housing through various forms of non-profit agency. This is the second arm of what is usually referred to as "social" housing. Some examples will indicate the diverse range of organisational structures, activities and financing arrangements that are found among these forms of housing supplier.

Non-profit housing enterprises have traditionally played an important role in the Federal Republic of Germany. Two-thirds of publicly assisted dwellings and one quarter of rented dwellings belong to these organisations.

In Canada, the stock of non-profit and/or cooperative housing owned by charitable organisations, at 180 thousand units, is almost as large as the stock of public housing owned by the Federal government. In recent years, dissatisfaction with the social imbalance and stigmatising effect of public housing has led the government to concentrate its policies for the assistance of low income groups on the expansion of the non profit rental housing sector. In this sector, attempts are made to attract tenants from a wider range of social backgrounds by ensuring that a maximum of 15 to 30 per cent of tenants from low income groups are accommodated in any one development. Most of the finance for non profit housing is provided by private financial institutions although the government offers interest rate subsidies which serve to reduce the cost of finance to about 2 per cent.

The Netherlands' government offers assistance to institutions supplying non profit rental housing on a comparable basis to that provided for public housing. That is, capital market loans are guaranteed by the government in return for control over the quality of accommodation. Rent subsidies are also offered. These are calculated in terms of the difference between the discounted annual rent that would be necessary to cover the full costs of the housing over a 50 year period and the basic rent level set by the government.

In the United Kingdom, non profit housing associations expanded their activities rapidly during the 70s. And although they only represent about 5 per cent of the total housing stock, the sharp decline in investment expenditure on new public housing since 1979 has meant that, in recent years, investment by housing associations has represented approximately half of total investment expenditure on social housing. The associations receive a range of capital and operating subsidies from central government. These are administered through the Housing Corporation which monitors and oversees the operation of individual associations. Rents are set at the regulated levels that apply in the regulated private rental sector.

Finally, Mediterranean countries such as Greece -- which does not have an established tradition of social housing -- have recently been encouraging the expansion of a wide spectrum of new activities and agencies, especially in connection with urban reinvestment. Figuring prominently among these have been "mixed economy" corporations based upon a combination of local public and private capital, and intermediate organisations such as housing cooperatives.

One of the main advantages claimed for non-profit organisations over public housing suppliers is that they have greater flexibility: this enables them to respond more rapidly to the changing housing environment. In part, this results from their small scale of operation. In this sense the difference is similar to that between a small sized firm with a limited management hierarchy and a large corporation with a lengthy line of management in either the public or the private sector. With a small scale of operation, it is argued, there is more scope for new initiatives and enterprise.

It is also claimed that housing associations were first to pioneer the decentralised systems of management, and policies that are responsive to tenants' wishes, which are currently being introduced into the public housing sector. Moreover, on the important question of finance, non profit organisations, which have long been dependent on both public and private sector finance, are well placed to engage in the form of public/private sector partnership schemes that tighter restraints on public expenditure suggest will become more commonplace in the future. At the same time, however, their continued reliance on public funding, will mean that their expansion will place added responsibilities on public sector bodies to make sure that money is spent in an efficient and equitable manner. In this connection, it is worth pointing out that the Canadian method for producing social mix in non profit housing developments that was mentioned above, has recently come under some criticisms for being insuffiently targeted on low income households. Once again there is a delicate balance to be drawn between conflicting policy objectives.


NOTE


1.  In this context the term "public" housing is used to refer to housing which is owned and managed by some level of government or one of its agencies. The next section of this chapter deals with non-profit housing associations and co-operatives; those are often heavily dependent on government funds and sometimes subject to direct government controls. Together these two sectors constitute what is often referred to as "social" housing. In much of this report, public housing, non-profit housing associations and co-operatives have been referred to collectively as social housing. In this chapter, however, a distinction has been drawn between public housing and private, non-profit housing. This distinction is sometimes blurred and does not apply uniformly to all countries. However, there are certain differences between the problems facing these two types of housing that are relevant to the discussion in this chapter.

Chapter VI

## HOUSING REINVESTMENT STRATEGIES

Reinvestment is a term employed by the Project Group to cover the range of expenditures aimed at maintaining and/or upgrading the quality of the existing housing stock. It includes expenditures on maintenance, renovation, rehabilitation and modernisation, as well as urban renewal.

In most OECD countries there is now an aggregate surplus of dwellings over households. As a result of this surplus, policy emphasis has shifted from the pursuit of quantitative targets to the pursuit of qualitative ones. In countries where there are substantial stocks of sub-standard housing, this shift of priorities has led to the growth of policies for reinvestment in the existing housing stock.

Possibly more than any of the other policy issues dealt with in this report, reinvestment is concerned directly with urban areas. It is within cities that the major problems are concentrated and policy responses required. But the incidence of sub standard housing and amenities is not spread evenly between cities: it is the larger and older cities that have a disproportionate share. Moreover, within such cities there are often marked spatial concentrations of sub-standard housing conditions. As a result re-investment policies often require a specific neighbourhood focus.

Reinvestment in the existing housing stock is not a new policy approach in all countries. In the United States, for example, housing modernisation and its area impacts were dealt with in the 1935 Housing Act. And, in the United Kingdom, "home improvement" grants for private dwellings were introduced in the 1949 Housing Act. But, despite these examples, at least up until the mid-70s, all countries were mainly concerned with the level of new construction work. However, with the emergence of the broad balance between household numbers and dwellings the emphasis changed. This is reflected in the marked increase in the share of reinvestment expenditure in total government spending in the United States and most Western European countries in the 80s.

It is not, however, only the change in aggregate household/dwelling numbers that have led to this shift of emphasis. At least three other factors have played a part. First, it reflects a considered response on the part of central and city governments to the urban and fiscal conditions that have emerged in recent years. To be specific, such policies are often a cost effective means of meeting the demand for good quality housing in the face of changing patterns of demand and rising real costs of construction. Also a given budget allocation can often distribute benefits more widely if it is used for reinvestment purposes, because the cost per unit is less than in the case of rebuilding. In times of scarce resources this may be considered to be more equitable than the concentration of larger per capita benefits on a smaller number of households, particularly if some of the major shortages of accommodation have been overcome. Further, there is often more scope for attracting additional private finance into areas of substandard housing through "pump priming" re-investment expenditure than is possible through rebuilding.

The second factor which has led to the increased emphasis on reinvestment has been the recognition of the adverse social consequences that have often resulted from demolition and rebuilding projects. These programmes have frequently led to the destruction of established communities, especially when older housing has been replaced by large scale, social housing estates. The vogue for high rise building has had particularly adverse social consequences in a number of countries. Moreover, the demolition process, with its legacy of blighted buildings and derelict land has often produced extensive negative externalities which have destabilised adjoining neighbourhoods.

Finally, in some countries, reinvestment has been seen as a policy capable of addressing specific national or local policy concerns more efficiently than rebuilding can do. Its role in promoting energy efficient strategies and/or making maximum use of scarce urban land provide examples of this emphasis.

At the same time, it has to be recognised that reinvestment strategies have not yet assumed the importance described above in Southern European countries such as Greece, Spain, Portugal and Turkey. Often, in these countries, the policies are of recent origin, confined to a small number of cities and still effectively on a demonstration scale. They represent an addition to existing policies aimed at new construction and, as such, form a far smaller part of total public expenditure on housing. In Greece, for example, maintenance and modernisation expenditure constitutes less than 10 per cent of total expenditure. Nonetheless it is likely that the pressures for a wider spread of these programmes will gather force in these countries just as they have done in the more industrialised countries in recent years.

The distinction between the approaches to housing investment found in the older, industrialised countries of Northern Europe and North America and the Mediterranean countries is just one aspect of the widely varying conditions found in OECD countries. In fact, even within countries there are usually important differences between areas of substandard housing, and these require different policy responses. In view of this diversity, this chapter has two main aims:

1. To identify the different causes of housing decay.

2. To identify the different reinvestment and other strategies that are appropriate for dealing with each type.

# CAUSES OF HOUSING DECAY

There are two distinct categories of substandard housing found in the urban areas dealt with in this report. On the one hand, there are concentrations of older, privately-owned, inner-city housing that have experienced long run decline; on the other hand, there are areas of public or social housing -- both within the inner-city and in suburban locations -- which have experienced accelerated decay.

## A. Deterioration in the Private Sector

The process of inner city decline within urban areas in older, industrialised countries is well known. Neighbourhoods pass through a predictable cycle as changes on both the supply and demand side of the market lead to a downward spiral in housing and neighbourhood conditions.

The cycle is set in motion as dwellings age and deteriorate. Of course, age, in itself, does not necessarily lead to substandard housing conditions; but the rate of depreciation does tend to increase exponentially with the age of a dwelling. As a consequence, the costs of repair and maintenance increase more rapidly than in the case of newer housing. In the absence of government policies which counteract the rising costs of accelerating depreciation, the relative costs of older housing rise. In addition, the standards of construction and amenity prevailing at the time when much of the older housing was built frequently no longer meet present day requirements. Sometimes modernisation can overcome this problem but it often tends to be expensive in comparison with modern, purpose built dwellings.

While the increasing relative cost of older, inner city housing has decreased the demand for it, other developments have taken place which have re-inforced this trend towards demand deficiency. In many cities transport improvements have provided easier access to the central city employment locations from the suburbs, while industrial restructuring has led to the decentralisation of many job locations. Moreover, changing housing preferences on the part of many young families have tended to favour newer housing at lower densities in suburban locations. As a result, there has been substantial out migration on the part of many middle and higher income households.

Following this out migration, levels of owner occupation have tended to fall within the inner city areas as properties have been converted to rental uses for lower income groups. Those in low wage occupations, the young, the unemployed, the elderly dependent on limited retirement pensions, and groups dependent on social welfare programmes are all among those making up an increasing proportion of households in these areas. However, because of their limited purchasing power low income households have rarely been able to afford the quantity of housing owned by the out movers. Moreover, household sizes have tended to fall as families have been replaced by both young and elderly single person households. Consequently as dwellings have filtered down they have usually been subdivided into smaller units. This has often resulted in multiple occupation and overcrowding. In many cases this has increased the rate of deterioration.

It is also important to note that the rate of deterioration has often been accentuated by the interdependence of investment decisions resulting from the existence of neighbourhood externalities. In many areas, property owners have been deterred from undertaking reinvestment expenditures because of their lack of confidence in the future of the area. A general decline in neighbourhood conditions, which reduces the desirability of an area, can prevent an owner from receiving an acceptable rate of return on his individual investment. This results in the well known "prisoner's dilemma" in which all property owners underinvest because of a lack of confidence in each other's behaviour. The intrusion of commercial and other incompatible land users into erstwhile residential areas can also be a source of negative externalities.

While particular circumstances have obviously varied from country to country, aspects of the cycle of decline described above have been experienced very widely. Possibly, they have been most pronounced in the United States where there has been a vicious circle of declining housing conditions in many inner city areas. Often these areas have been completely abandoned by the white middle classes and now comprise almost totally low income, ethnic minority households. In the Netherlands also, the density, structural defects, lack of modern facilities, parking and open spaces associated with inner city housing built during the period of rapid industrialisation have resulted in the out migration of those households that can afford to do so. Inner city populations have now stabilised in terms of aggregate numbers but the composition has changed with a large growth in the share of old and low income groups. Luxembourg has experienced trends similar to those of the Netherlands. In Japan a slightly different manifestation of the out migration process has been noted. Here, as elsewhere, dissatisfaction with inner city housing conditions has led to out migration to the newer suburbs with lower densities and higher environmental standards. This has not, however, tended to produce decay in the inner cities but, rather, high vacancy rates.

So far the process of housing decay has been presented as the consequence of various market processes; however, it is imortant to realise that a number of government policy instruments have contributed to the process insofar as they have acted to deter maintenance expenditure. The three major ones have been rent control, tax expenditures offered to owner occupiers and the growth of subsidised social housing.

Rent Control

Within large OECD cities the rental sector commonly represents 60-75 per cent of the housing stock. In older neighbourhoods, the share of private sector rental housing is particularly pronounced. Chapter V has already described how rent control, by reducing the rate of return available to the landlord, has reduced the incentive to undertake maintenance expenditure. The cumulative neglect of this expenditure has clearly accelerated the rate of housing decay in many areas.

Tax Expenditures

In some countries (e.g. Germany, Sweden and the United States), tax policies -- by allowing accelerated depreciation of modernisation investment against taxable income -- have stimulated investment in the private rental sector. But generally, the widespread use of tax expenditures to stimulate

85

owner occupation (see Chapter III) has meant that their impact on inner city neighbourhoods has been deleterious. This has resulted from three main factors. First, the incidence of owner occupation in the inner city is lower than elsewhere and often declining. Second, those owners remaining in the inner city usually receive lower per capita tax reliefs because of, _inter alia_, the low value of their properties, the high deposit to loan ratios required of them, and the fact that many of them are elderly, outright owners with no mortgage debt on which to attract tax relief. And third, systems of tax relief have tended to encourage middle income households into higher valued property in suburban areas and away from depreciated structures in the older housing areas.

### Social Housing

In those countries where subsidised, social housing has been developed, it has often been more attractive to tenants on grounds of both cost and quality than the private rental sector. This alternative has obviously reduced the demand for private rental housing.

There are, therefore, multiple causes of decline in inner city, private housing stocks and policies designed to rejuvenate these areas will need to be formulated on the basis of a clear understanding of these diverse factors and the inter-dependencies between them.

Finally, although the diversity of experiences among OECD countries was stressed at the outset of this chapter, it is important to reiterate that not all countries have suffered this decline of the inner city. For example, Australia, Finland, New Zealand and Sweden have comparatively recent housing stocks built to high standards of construction and amenity. In these countries general environmental quality tends to be high and market failure is less evident. Nonetheless, even these countries are concerned to devise reinvestment policies for the future to avoid the problems manifested in those countries which have experienced inner city decline.

### B. Decline in Areas of Social Housing

In the majority of countries the proportion of the dwelling stock represented by social housing tends to be significantly higher than the national average in large cities. In the United Kingdom, for example, the national share is just below 30 per cent whereas in cities with populations of over a half a million the share is near 50 per cent. Moreover, at the urban level, there is a tendency for social housing to be built in large, single tenure tracts. Few countries have adopted the Canadian strategy of dispersing social housing through the purchase of units in private developments. Generally, therefore, areas of social housing are characterised by their spatial concentration and homogeneity.

Prior to the 70s the problems of cumulative disrepair in the condition of social housing was not a major policy issue. In consequence systematic modernisation policies barely existed. Central governments provided local agencies minimal advice on best practice and, as a result, maintenance policies displayed significant local variations. Of course there were differences between countries manifested in variations in maintenance expenditure. For example, spending in Sweden was already quite high; in the

Netherlands and in the United Kingdom it was more modest; and in France it was relatively low.

As has been mentioned previously, at this time most governments were preoccupied with the construction of new social housing rather than reinvestment. By the mid-70s, with new building still at high levels, rises in interest rates made the financing of social housing more problematic. Furthermore, housing maintenance and management costs (which are both labour intensive activities) tended to rise more rapidly than the general price level following the increased rates of wage inflation that resulted from the first oil price shock. At the time tenants were receiving substantial rent subsidies and rises in rents were often problematic politically. The financing problems facing social housing were then exacerbated as governments sought to restrict the growth in public expenditure generally by cuts in housing budgets. It was within this scenario that already modest levels of maintenance expenditure became the target of economies.

These budgetary pressures have continued into the 80s. At the same time, repair requests have increased in many countries. This has meant an increase in repair backlogs and delivery times in many areas of social housing. In part this may be a reaction on the tenants' part to rising rent levels, but it is also a predictable outcome of the long term deterioration of older social housing in the absence of a systematic maintenance policy. What has been less predictable, though, has been the extent to which, in some areas, social housing that has been constructed since the 60s has begun to exhibit alarmingly high levels of technological obsolescence and serious social shortcomings. Hence, there are two categories of social housing, each of which has been the subject of rather different causes and processes of decline; older, pre-1960 dwellings and the more recent, post-1960 built housing.

### Older Social Housing

Older social housing is an important source of accommodation in most Western European countries. Some of it, in the Netherlands for example, predates the first World War; in Britain and France it also has a long vintage becoming an important source of supply from 1920 onwards. Because of the date of its construction, areas of this type of housing are usually nearer the centre of urban areas than more recently built social housing estates, and are, therefore, less segregated spatially. However, given the age of much of the dwelling stock, it is not surprising that it is currently posing a number of problems for social housing agencies. In particular three sources of concern are discernable in a number of countries.

First, there has been the age related depreciation of the stock discussed already. However, because the generally accepted standard of minimum housing need is income elastic, expectations of dwelling characteristics have been increased over time beyond the level initially provided in this type of housing. Thus, in Sweden, it is now regarded as essential that blocks of flats contain lifts for the elderly and people with disabilities, that modern energy conservation standards are met, that effective refuse collection and disposal systems are installed, and that more generous modern space standards are met.

A second set of concerns relates to the level of amenities provided within the neighbourhood areas. Nursery schools, health care centres and community facilities are now all widely recognised as being an integral part of the living environment. All too frequently the single sector approach to city planning in the past meant that there were serious gaps in amenity provision within easy access of areas of social housing.

A third concern is that resident populations in these areas have undergone compositional changes over the years which has resulted in social imbalance. This has arisen because many of these areas have been popular neighbourhoods offering housing at generally subsidised rent levels, at least until more recent systems of income related housing allowances have been introduced in a number of countries. As a result, established households have had little incentive to move and have aged in situ. This has produced heavy concentrations of elderly households. More recently, some of these areas have witnessed the growth of long term unemployed populations as inner city employment prospects have contracted. In general though, these social problems are less acute than in areas of more recently built social housing. In some ways this is because the very proximity of these areas to the city means that they are less socially isolated. In general they do not, therefore, require wholesale neighbourhood reinvestment; but they do require dwelling modernisation, attention to amenity provision and more efficient and generous maintenance programmes.

## Recently Built Social Housing

By the late 70s a number of countries that had pursued vigorous rehousing policies over the period 1960-75 were facing a very sharp decline in the environmental quality and social and economic characteristics of certain modern, social housing estates. In retrospect, it is evident that these processes had a number of common causes:

-- The newer estates were developed very rapidly as slum housing was demolished;

-- The large scale of development necessitated easy land assembly and this tended to bias development to peripheral locations leading to social dislocation;

-- Investment decisions were usually made without any tenant input on questions of design;

-- Under the influence of architects and central government subsidies geared to the minimisation of short run development costs, these estates contained many high rise units; once again, adverse social consequences resulted from this design form;

-- Non-traditional forms of building were associated with the use of non-traditional materials and systems which have subsequently revealed major design failings e.g. flat roofs that failed to shed rainwater, cladding pads secured with ferrous pins that rusted rapidly, steel frame windows that also rusted, insubstantial interior divisions that failed to insulate noise adequately, materials that suffered from differential expansion cracks, etc.

-- There was a planning obsession with the number of dwelling units and a disregard for the provision of complementary amenities;

-- Dwellings were designed with extensive common space which was intended to facilitate social integration; however, subsequent experience suggests that this is more often a source of vandalism, and that tenants prefer a greater amount of private, defensible space.

Design problems, lack of amenity, peripheral location, incipient disrepair and social dislocation often all coupled with higher rent levels than tenants experienced elsewhere have resulted in the unpopularity of these estates. Those tenants who could, left these areas and were typically higher income households. Outmovers have been replaced by poor, socially disadvantaged and ethnic minority households with little freedom of choice.

The French "grand ensemble" of "Les Minguettes" on the southern outskirts of the conurbation of Lyon provides a vivid example of the process of decline suffered by modern, social housing estates. Les Minguettes was built in three separate stages, the first one dating from 1968. Ten different public housing companies (Habitation à Loyer Modéré -- HLM) were involved in the production of 7 400 social housing units and 1 200 private or co-ownership units. The population of the municipality within which it is situated, Venissieux, grew from 30 thousand to 65 thousand over the period. Its housing stock is comprised exclusively of densely developed five and ten storey blocks. In physical terms the dwelling units were, and in some cases still are, of substantial quality, although dampness is a common problem.

At first the dwellings were let as soon as they were completed, invariably to "Metropolitan French" residents in employment. After a time, however, part of the area declined in popularity: a ten tower block area (Monmousseau) experienced a fall in the number of households from 550 to 220 in just under two years. This led to a spread in the pattern of abandonment in other areas of the grand ensemble. Between 1981 and 1985 vacancies grew from under 1 500 to nearly 2 500. The high vacancy rate and increased rate of turnover led to a change in the composition of in movers. In 1983/84, for example, 50 per cent of entrants were "non Metropolitan French," 40 per cent had no earner in the household and 10 per cent were single parent families. In addition, existing tenants in poorer zones quickly applied for vacancies in blocks that were perceived as "better" quality. Thus internal transfers heightened the concentration of vacancies and diverted new comers to the worst blocks.

Les Minguettes is now characterised by deteriorating buildings and environmental fabric (lifts often do not work, open spaces have been vandalised), high vacancy rates, growing numbers of low income and ethnic minority households, and problems associated with drugs, violence and suicide. With vandalism, maintenance costs per property have risen 25 per cent above those identical properties, for the same HLM, in other parts of the Lyon conurbation. But Les Minguettes is not unique. It is an example of a world wide urban problem that requires urgent attention from policy makers. Important efforts are now being made both on the part of the national and local government to upgrade Les Minguettes and to change its image.

STRATEGIES FOR REINVESTMENT IN PRIVATE SECTOR HOUSING

Policies designed to upgrade areas of substandard private housing may take a variety of forms. And although most programmes found in OECD countries contain a mix of policy instruments, it is possible to distinguish two main categories of approach. On the one hand, there are policies which seek to "lubricate" the market system by encouraging individual property owners to undertake re-investment expenditures. Alternatively, there are more broadly based area and/or intersectoral approaches which usually entail a more "collective" approach.

## A. Individual Based Programmes

Programmes centred on individual decision makers endeavour to stimulate re-investment activity by increasing the ease of access to, and rate of return on, reinvestment expenditure. The main methods which are used to do this are offers of low interest loans, grants and tax subsidies.

Loans for housing re-investment expenditure at below market interest rates are available in many countries (e.g. Australia, Canada, Finland, France, Greece, Japan, Spain, Sweden and the United States). Often these are part of an overall finance policy designed to stimulate housing investment in general. But in some countries reinvestment expenditure attracts specifically favourable treatment. In France, for example, private landlords can under certain circumstances receive subsidised loans which defray about 30 per cent of modernisation costs. In Spain too subsidised loans are available to landlords and owners undertaking modernisation work in the private sector.

In many cases loan subsidies are combined with grants towards modernisation expenditure. Again in France, for instance, grants of up to 20 per cent of the total cost of work are available for both landlords and owner occupiers who wish to bring their housing up to modern health, safety and amenity standards. In addition, grants of up to 50 per cent are available for specific sanitary improvements. Luxembourg also provides small grants based on a percentage value of the improvement work undertaken; this is also available to tenants who finance work themselves. Moreover, if the tenant's own labour is used, the cost of this may be included in the claim. It is, though, in the United Kingdom that grants for private repair and improvement work have probably been used most extensively -- to the exclusion of other reinvestment instruments.

In the United Kingdom, as part of a predominantly centrally funded programme, individual owners can apply to local government for repair or improvement grants to undertake necessary repairs, provide basic amenities or upgrade the quality of their dwelling. The maximum percentage of the total cost that can be offered to an owner has been varied between 50 and 90 per cent at different times and in different areas. The grants are not income related and eligibility is a function of property condition and the "rateable" value of the property (i.e. its assessed value for property tax purposes, although the 90 per cent grant is usually only available to "hardship" cases). There was a rapid increase in expenditure on improvement grants following the more generous provisions of the 1981 Housing Act. Between 1980/81 and 1983/84, real expenditure increased over fivefold. More recently the size of the programme has been scaled down. In fact, the government, no doubt alarmed by the scale of the increase in expenditure, and the possibility that a large part of this expenditure might merely be substituting public money for private money, has discussed the scope for greater targeting through the introduction of means tests for grant applicants, and the use of repayable loans as a subsitute for grants in the case of higher income applicants. But no firm measures are presently planned along these lines.

Tax expenditures represent yet another means of subsidising private reinvestment expenditure. In those countries where owner occupation is subject to tax on imputed income (see Table 13), it is usual to allow deductions for reinvestment expenditures. Similar arrangements also, of course, apply to private landlords' reinvestment expenditures. In those countries where no tax is applied to imputed income, but where mortgage loan interest payments are able to be set against general income tax liability, it is normal to allow some tax deductibility on reinvestment expenditures.

By reducing the private costs of reinvestment expenditure, low interest loans, grants and tax expenditures endeavour to overcome the impediments to housing improvements caused by various forms of market failure. While each of these instruments has had some success in conserving certain sections of the housing stock, they have rarely been sufficiently strong to reverse extreme forms of spatially concentrated housing disinvestment. To reverse these trends, more comprehensive programmes are usually called for.

## B. Comprehensive Reinvestment Programmes

Comprehensive programmes may be based upon either "market related" or "buyout" strategies.

### Market related strategies

This approach tends to rely upon similar instruments to those offered via individual-based subsidy programmes, viz loans and grants; however, the subsidies are targeted in a far more spatially specific fashion. The aim is usually to concentrate assistance on well defined, contiguous plots of substandard housing in the hope that favourable neighbourhood effects will lead to housing revitalisation through the market process. Just as negative neighbourhood externalities play an important part in the process of cumulative neighbourhood decline, so in some cases, area improvement can be self sustaining.

In fact, this prospect has already been observed in a number of cities in Europe and North America where economic and demographic changes have interacted to raise the demand for dwellings in inner city areas. Demographic changes, influenced in part by economic change, have led to new patterns of household formation (see Chapter I). More adults remain single longer and more never marry; young households tend to delay starting families longer; there are more small households formed by divorce and separation; and there are more single and two person elderly households. These trends have all resulted in greater demand for smaller dwellings.

Many of the older, inner city areas have supplies of small housing units that satisfy these demands. At the same time, rising transport costs and renewed preferences for the accessibility offered by central city

91

locations have added to the demand. Thus, even with quite low levels of subsidy, inmovers have been prepared to undertake substantial modernisation expenditures if there is potential for property and neighbourhood improvement.

On a more negative note, there is concern that this process -- generally known as "gentrification" -- sometimes leads to the displacement of lower income households. As middle income improvers move in, there is greater competition for the available housing and a reduction in the supply of low income accommodation. The process can, therefore, have regressive income redistributional consequences. More generally though, market led incentives have given cause for concern because they simply have not led to the scale of area improvement that governments have sought to promote. This has led to the more widespread adoption of buy-out strategies.

## "Buyout Strategies"

In some OECD countries central governments have developed a framework of enabling legislation to allow buyout strategies (e.g. Portugal and the Netherlands). These usually permit a municipality or social housing agency to acquire tracts of private, sub-standard housing with a view to organising and financing the reinvestment itself on an integrated basis. These strategies are usually necessary when the level of disinvestment and the incidence of negative external effects make individual initiatives most unlikely.

In the formulation of effective buyout strategies three important issues need to be resolved. These are:

1. The method of funding of the modernisation agency;

2. The relative cost effectiveness of the strategy; and

3. The rent setting procedures to be used for post-buyout tenants.

The funding of localised buyouts is usually borne ultimately by central government, although in some cases municipal taxes are expected to contribute up to 10 per cent of total costs. The central funds are normally allocated to local governments who have freedom to determine expenditures -- within limits -- in the light of their local knowledge of housing needs. In some cases, the funds are directed through social housing agencies, such as Housing Associations in the United Kingdom. Under both organisational forms, however, the municipality usually assumes a key role in project planning and in co-ordinating housing investment with other local services and investments required for neighbourhood revitalisation.

Because buyouts involve central government funding and local government expenditure, it is usual to find centrally specified cost and standard guidelines for reinvestment expenditures. Most central governments specify a cut-off point for modernisation in terms of the relevant cost of new construction. In France, for example, rehabilitation is not normally financed if its cost would exceed 75 per cent of the new construction cost. In the Netherlands a rather more generous cut off point of 90 per cent is used. In some countries, where reinvestment policy is developed with a view to conserving historic central city areas, the special value attached to the preservation of the traditional environment, and the higher cost of building traditional building forms, leads to the adoption of cut off points of about 100 per cent.

However, although these cut off rules are administratively simple, they are no substitute for more systematic appraisal. Very few countries have well developed evaluative procedures. Although many governments adopt reinvestment strategies because of their belief in the external or social benefits that result from this form of expenditure -- in addition to the benefits that accrue directly to residents enjoying superior housing -- little use is made of techniques designed to measure these effects, such as cost-benefit analysis. While there is little doubt that such schemes boost confidence in the affected areas, little is known in precise quantitative terms about the magnitude of spillovers or the social rates of return on different components of reinvestment packages.

Finally, buyout strategies need to establish rent setting criteria. Generally, even after allowing for central government subsidisation, most modernised properties require substantial increases in rent levels to cover their costs. However, it is usual to ameliorate the impact of rent increases in a number of ways. In Rotterdam, for example, the municipality "pools" rents across its entire stock. In other countries, e.g. Portugal and the United Kingdom, there is an increasing tendency to set rents that approximate market levels while offering tenants income related housing allowances. In this way, the displacement of existing tenants can be reduced.

## C. Intersectoral Reinvestment Policies

Although market-related and buyout reinvestment strategies both represent a direct response to the problems of deteriorating housing stocks, it is now widely recognised that these areas are but one symptom of wider social and economic decline. Accordingly, in many countries, housing reinvestment programmes have been supplemented by other policies which go beyond investment in the built environment. These "intersectoral" policies attempt to confront the multiplicity of physical, economic and social causes of decay.

In the Netherlands, for example, urban regeneration policies in the major industrial areas suffering from economic and social decline are based upon economic development and job creation programmes. These are combined with other spatially targeted welfare programmes. And, in turn, these are coordinated with housing reinvestment measures through the town planning system. The United States also uses an inter sectoral approach through its Urban Development Action Grants. These are provided in areas of high unemployment and economic depression. Once again, though, their focus goes beyond the housing market, as they aim to meet economic and welfare objectives as well. As part of its national planning process, France has declared an explicit objective to "improve the quality of urban life." As part of the strategy designed to meet this objective, 15 joint national-regional programmes have been established. These cover such aspects as industrial restructuring, training and retraining, job creation and environmental improvement. Housing reinvestment is seen as just one of the components of these programmes. In the United Kingdom, the Urban Programme provides additional resources from central government funds for areas with special needs. In most cases these are declining inner city areas with decayed infrastructure and poor environmental quality; they are also usually areas of high population loss, higher than average rates of unemployment and high concentrations of welfare dependent households. In short, they are areas of multiple deprivation. The Urban Programme seeks to stimulate economic regeneration with the expectation that one of the consequences will be housing reinvestment and environmental improvement. In pursuing these strategies local governments are encouraged to involve the private sector and to pay special attention to the needs of ethnic minorities.

These intersectoral policy initiatives are still in their infancy in most countries. Once again there is, at the moment, a lack of hard evidence about the precise costs and benefits arising from different forms of expenditure. However, preliminary indications suggest that housing reinvestment does have favourable employment generating effects in its own right. As a labour intensive activity, expenditure on housing reinvestment can produce significant reductions in local unemployment rates; although the size of the employment multiplier will depend upon expenditure leakages from the targeted area. For example, in Glasgow most firms involved in reinvestment and their workforces reside in the city. In Rotterdam, in contrast, while reinvestment strategies use local firms it is estimated that 60 per cent of employees live in the suburbs or new towns.

In addition to the short term employment generating effects of reinvestment expenditures, it is important to establish whether the longer term economic base of an urban area can be enhanced by them. It is now well known that firms' location decisions are influenced by the quality of life offered by different environments. Once again, Glasgow provides a good example of the potential here. For many years the city suffered from a depressed image and was not seen as an attractive location by management from, particularly, the South East of England. More recently, however, the image of the city has been improved and high level executives are now more willing to move there. Microelectronics, fashion and even the film industry have been attracted to the city. This experience provides an encouraging example of the way in which housing modernisation, undertaken with quite high levels of initial public sector subsidy, can stimulate private residential reinvestment and, ultimately, have a positive long run effect on the local economic base.

In concluding this discussion of reinvestment policies towards private sector housing, it is worth reiterating that governments in OECD countries have shown a growing awareness of the need for this type of expenditure. As a result, policies have been developed to facilitate reinvestment, both by lubricating the market and, in more extreme cases, by replacing it through buyouts. However, with very few exceptions, there has been far less attention given to the development of policies designed to encourage continuing maintenance expenditure by owners. This is, of course, a major oversight as it is the neglect of this expenditure in the past that has led to many of the present day problems, and which, if neglected now, will result in the recurrence of these problems in the future.


REINVESTMENT POLICIES FOR SOCIAL HOUSING


At the beginning of the 80s it became clear that traditional rehabilitation strategies were not producing the desired scale of improvement in those countries experiencing accelerated decay in the social housing sector. As a consequence of these failings, a range of new initiatives -- such as those represented by the "Commission nationale pour le développement social des quartiers", which by 1986 covered 120 large development schemes in France, and the Priority Estates Project, which covered 90 housing estates in the United Kingdom -- have been developed. Although the emphasis and form of these initiatives varies somewhat between countries, there are certain features common to the new style approach.

Generally there is an emphasis on the decentralisation of responsibilities. Experience suggests that both general housing management functions, and the specific management of reinvestment strategies, are best devolved to the local level. This involves assigning a greater role to local authorities who can be expected to have a better knowledge of the precise pattern of local needs than central government. In addition, devolution also means the decentralisation of management functions within local authority areas to administrative levels that are more accessible to tenants. Increasing tenant participation in decision making is emphasised both in terms of eliciting their preferences about the forms of reinvestments affecting their dwellings directly and also in more general terms in relation to proposed repair policies, environmental improvement schemes, management practices, etc. By giving tenants greater control over their own living environments, the new initiatives seek to tap the considerable stock of dormant human resources which, through personal initiative and community involvement, can greatly assist the revitalisation of blighted, social housing estates.

The decentralisation of functions is clearly a means of making the providers of social housing more accountable to the preferences of individual tenants. In this way it should prevent the recurrence of some of the major planning disasters of the 60s when large scale, high rise estates -- which met architectural and financial requirements, but were social disasters for the people who actually had to live in them -- were the favoured form of construction. However, the public finance needed to facilitate reinvestment strategies will need to be provided by higher tiers of government, typically central government, which have greater revenue raising capacities and the scope for revenue sharing between rich and poor areas. The division of revenue raising and spending functions represented by this system of "bottom up" budget requests and "top down" funding raises the issue of the appropriate form of central-local government finance arrangements.

At the moment most countries employ a set of reinvestment finance instruments which are similar to those used to encourage private sector reinvestment expenditure. Hence, for example, in France, the Netherlands and Sweden, central government offers subsidised loans. Municipal housing companies and housing associations can fund modernisation with loans between 2 and 5 per cent below the market rate, with payback periods of up to 30 years. Outright grants for specific purposes are also commonly available. These arrangements are fairly longstanding. However, with the development of more active, locally based strategies, which often involve more heavy subsidisation of specifically targeted areas, some new pressures may arise. This is because central government can be expected to determine the aggregate scale of subsidisation to particular local authorities, who then have the autonomy to allocate the given quantity of resources in ways which they deem appropriate. This system can be expected to work well if central and local governments share a common perception of the desirable quantity of aggregate resources, and agree on the broad lines of local allocation, but where this condition is not met it may become a source of considerable political tension.

Another aspect of financing policy which distinguishes the new approach to reinvestment in social housing is the attempt to attract private finance into this area. In both the United Kingdom and the United States the private sector has become involved in reinvestment schemes through a number of joint public-private sector initiatives. Sometimes, as in the case of the private sector reinvestment, this may involve the provision of credit finance by lending institutions which have not traditionally extended their activities to these areas. Often, though, the private sector participation is even more direct with private developers purchasing and remodeling particular stocks of social housing. In the United Kingdom, under the Urban Development Grants Scheme, local authorities and private developers come together to jointly devise redevelopment proposals which are submitted to central government for grant aid. Similar methods of "leveraging" private sector funds are used in Australia. Non profit housing associations and cooperatives also typically play a part in these schemes.

Where it is successful, the mixed pattern of development and ownership that is produced by these partnership schemes reduces the extent of social segregation suffered by some social housing estates. By increasing the heterogeneity of tenure types and the socio-economic composition of the areas, they are less likely to be residualised. It is, however, sometimes claimed that there is a danger of the displacement of low income households in these schemes, especially if they are unable to meet the higher rent payments that private finance often requires.

In fact, the available evidence suggests that the displacement of tenants because of rent increases has not been a serious problem in most redevelopment schemes. This is because a series of subsidy mechanisms have been used to moderate the increased costs borne by individual tenants. First, as has already been described, central government subsidised loans and grants are usually available. In France, the Netherlands and the United Kingdom as much as 50 per cent of the cost of major schemes may be defrayed in this way. Second, social housing agencies have the opportunity of "pooling" the costs of individual schemes across their entire housing stock. That is, the "averaging" of rents means that some tenants pays higher than cost rents to enable those in high cost areas to be charged less. If a social housing agency has a large proportion of its stock in areas undergoing reinvestment the scope for relieving tenants through pooling is limited. But, in general, pooling is an important mechanism by which the cost of reinvestment undertaken on poor stock is partly paid for by rent surplus generating estates. (In this connection it is worth noting that the decentralisation of finance to smaller administrative areas may limit the scope of pooling). Finally, the impact of increased rents is lessened by the introduction of income related housing allowances on many countries. (Once again, though, there is a potentially adverse side effect to this aspect of support: that is, it may serve to increase social segregation by attracting low income tenants, who are eligible for housing allowances, and deterring higher income households who are not). Overall, however, the ameliorating effects of subsidies, grants, pooling and housing allowances mean that tenants in social housing estates rarely face net rent increases of more than 25 per cent following redevelopment. And although this might seem a substantial increase in some contexts, it must be remembered that rents often start from an extremely low benchmark.

A final consideration that new approaches to reinvestment in social housing estates must face is the continuing need for repair and maintenance expenditure following initial reinvestment. This is vital to prevent the recurrence of accelerated decay in the future. In fact, in some countries, measures are already being implemented to improve the efficiency of repairs expenditure by including it within the general move towards decentralisation. Decentralised systems appear to make tenant reporting of repair requests simpler, ease the subsequent administrative contact and often reduce costs. In general, they tend to improve landlord-tenant relationships.

A recent report by the Audit Commission for England and Wales recommended the administrative decentralisation of the repairs service down to the level of approximately 7 000 units. This is, in fact, a similar size to many Swedish social housing companies and also equivalent to the organisational zones currently employed in the Netherlands. Public housing (HLM) operating in such areas as Les Minguettes is also moving in this direction: in many cases the ratio of caretakers -- who carry out simple repairs -- to units has been tripled.

The other main aspect of efficiency relating to repairs expenditure is obviously the level of efficiency achieved in the production of the work itself. Many countries arrange for this work to be carried out exclusively by public sector repair teams. However, there is some evidence that delays are reduced and the cost of the work is less if the work is put out to tender from both public and private sector agencies.


## THE PRIVATISATION OF SOCIAL HOUSING


Probably the most radical response to the problems of social housing is the one that has been adopted most forcefully by the British government: that is, the sale of social housing into owner occupation. This policy has also, of course, been pursued as a means of expanding owner occupation. Through the Housing Act, 1980 the Government transformed the terms of which Local Authorities (LA) were to sell their dwellings. Whereas sales had previously been at the discretion of individual LAs, the 1980 Act gave tenants a statutory right-to-buy. The LA had a mandatory obligation to sell if a tenant wished to buy. Moreover, dwellings were to be offered for purchase at a discount on the open market price, ranging from 33 per cent for a buyer who had been a tenant for less than 4 years, up to 50 per cent for tenants of 17 years or more standing. The maximum discount has subsequently been raised to 60 per cent.

Following the passage of the Act, the number of dwellings sold under the right-to-buy clause soared: from less than 80 thousand in 1980 to a peak of nearly 200 thousand in 1982. By 1986 nearly 20 per cent of the pre 1980 stock of LA housing had been sold to sitting tenants. The government is also investigating ways of transferring "blocks" of housing to private sector landlords.

97

Chapter VII

## GROUP RECOMMENDATIONS

### INTRODUCTION

There are wide variations in the housing systems and policies in OECD Member countries. But most of them have experienced difficulties in achieving the basic housing objectives of efficiency and equity. In particular historical development of housing finance and tax systems has led to a pattern of subsidies which obscures the real cost of housing.

At the moment many countries are in the process of reassessing their housing policies. The first task is to determine the appropriate role of central and local government in housing. Within their fiscal restrictions governments may wish to produce a more cohesive and consistent housing strategy to cover all tenures. This might be primarily designed to meet housing objectives rather than as a subsidiary component of other policies, e.g. employment or regional policies.

### NEW PRIORITIES

Rising incomes and changes in demographic composition have led to increased aspirations for smaller but higher quality dwellings in many OECD countries. There is an increasing trend for this to be met by the private market through new construction and adjustments to the existing stock.

Concern is shifting in many countries from the provision of new dwellings to maintenance, repair and improvement of existing dwellings. Governments may wish to consider whether their housing policies emphasise sufficiently both this need and the necessary stock adjustments.

In those countries still experiencing migration into urban areas and higher population growth, however, policies are likely to continue to focus on new construction.

Most housing policies are nationally-based, yet housing conditions and problems can differ significantly between regions within a country. Governments may wish to consider whether their systems offer sufficient flexibility to deal with the variety of regional problems encountered.

Revitalisation of urban areas is an increasing concern in many countries. Governments may wish to consider the extent to which the required reinvestment can be initiated by housing activities. Also attention needs to be devoted to the relative roles to be played by the public and private sectors, in partnership, in reviving confidence in an urban area.

Successful urban regeneration encompasses non-housing as well as housing reinvestment; this needs to be spatially concentrated in well-defined neighbourhoods. It is also desirable to decentralise public services. It is important that housing policies are consistent with this, and that they are supported by other activities, such as social and environmental improvement programmes, which allow for comprehensive area improvement.


# PRICING


In order to develop efficient housing policies governments have to be aware of the real cost of housing and aim towards a pricing structure which in general reflects these costs.

In the social housing sector too rent structures need to correspond more closely to the value of housing services provided by dwellings.

## Subsidies to Consumers

Housing, however, is an expensive commodity and most countries will wish to continue to limit the level of cost borne by consumers. Some countries will wish to maintain a broad-based support system.

Others may prefer a greater degree of targeting and selectivity. They may consider adapting their policies to achieve greater targeting in terms of some of the following criteria:

-- Households on low incomes;

-- Households wishing to enter or having recently entered the housing market such as first-time buyers, new entrants to the rental sector, etc.;

-- Households with special needs, e.g. people with handicaps, mental disabilities etc.;

-- Household expenditure on specific aspects of housing for which the social benefit is greater than the private benefit, e.g. energy saving features;

-- Households moving into or improving dwellings in areas undergoing revitalisation where the social benefit is greater than the private benefit.

It may be the case that the expansion of a particular tenure is the most efficient way of achieving a general housing or social objective. But countries may wish to consider whether there is a case for greater emphasis on tenure neutral approaches.

## Owner Occupation

In those countries seeking to achieve growth of owner occupation, special mortgage instruments such as deferred payment, index-linked and equity sharing mortgages can help to reduce the outlay of home owners in the first years and may have a greater role to play than they have to date. They will be of special help to families with modest incomes and help to defray the transaction costs associated with movement.

Some governments may wish to consider methods to improve the targeting of subsidies to home owners in order to contain their costs and reduce their other negative aspects. These could include restricting them to first time buyers; introducing a ceiling on tax relief; restricting the period of time over which it is available; introducing tax credits; or directing aid to home owners on low incomes.

## The Rental Sector

Some countries are concerned to encourage the growth, or maintain the size, of their rental sectors because of the advantages they offer by providing a tenure suitable to some households' circumstances and facilitating mobility.

### The Private Rental Sector

In the private rental sector this may best be achieved by the gradual decontrol of rents, for example decontrollings new lettings at a pace which allows the supply of housing to adjust and thereby avoids the incidence of windfall capital gains. This must not jeopardise security of tenure and may need to be supported by housing allowances. This strategy is most likely to achieve the necessary broad political consensus. Rent decontrol may also lessen the problems of disrepair and maintenance.

Within the private rental sector, arrangements which enable tenants to be consulted about the ways in which their housing is managed can also contribute to maintaining the quality of this housing.

### Public Rental Sector

In seeking to encourage the public rental sector, some countries may wish to adopt initiatives that are already underway elsewhere; these aim to improve management and to introduce more flexibility in setting rents and improving housing conditions, especially on large estates.

In response to criticisms of over centralised and bureaucratic management practices which do not respond sufficiently to tenants preferences, a number of countries are developing new management systems. These involve the decentralisation of functions, responsibilities and budgeting, and may incorporate a greater degree of tenant participation in decision making.

In some countries poor housing conditions and social problems are particularly acute in the large tracts of post war social housing. These may require a greater level of maintenance and reinvestment than is presently taking place. Countries may consider how best to achieve a more balanced mix of tenants on these estates. One means of integrating public housing tenants into the life of the city in a way that spatial segregation does not permit, is to build public housing in small scale developments at locations throughout the urban area. Another could be building or converting dwellings for private ownership on existing estates.

## Non-Profit Rental Sector

In countries where non-profit organisations have developed into large scale operations, their division into smaller units is favoured as a means of improving efficiency and accountability. Elsewhere small scale non-profit organisations may offer an attractive alternative tenure in the rental sector. They possess a number of features such as relative autonomy, using a combination of public and private finance, often decentralised management structures, and frequently incorporating tenant participation, which make them particularly suited to the changing housing situation.


CONCLUDING REMARKS


Many aspects of housing finance and tax systems have direct implications for urban development. Although there is a tendency for governments to decentralise responsibilities, there is nonetheless a continuing need for national governments to ensure consistency between housing policy and their objectives for cities. Due attention to these linkages is a necessary prerequisite of successful urban regeneration strategies and for ensuring an acceptable quality of life for people in urban areas.

# WHERE TO OBTAIN OECD PUBLICATIONS
## OÙ OBTENIR LES PUBLICATIONS DE L'OCDE

**ARGENTINA - ARGENTINE**
Carlos Hirsch S.R.L.,
Florida 165, 4° Piso,
(Galeria Guemes) 1333 Buenos Aires
Tel. 33.1787.2391 y 30.7122

**AUSTRALIA - AUSTRALIE**
D.A. Book (Aust.) Pty. Ltd.
11-13 Station Street (P.O. Box 163)
Mitcham, Vic. 3132        Tel. (03) 873 4411

**AUSTRIA - AUTRICHE**
OECD Publications and Information Centre,
4 Simrockstrasse,
5300 Bonn (Germany)        Tel. (0228) 21.60.45
Gerold & Co., Graben 31, Wien 1  Tel. 52.22.35

**BELGIUM - BELGIQUE**
Jean de Lannoy,
Avenue du Roi 202
B-1060 Bruxelles        Tel. (02) 538.51.69

**CANADA**
Renouf Publishing Company Ltd/
Éditions Renouf Ltée,
1294 Algoma Road, Ottawa, Ont. K1B 3W8
Tel: (613) 741-4333
Toll Free/Sans Frais:
Ontario, Quebec, Maritimes:
1-800-267-1805
Western Canada, Newfoundland:
1-800-267-1826
Stores/Magasins:
61 rue Sparks St., Ottawa, Ont. K1P 5A6
Tel: (613) 238-8985
211 rue Yonge St., Toronto, Ont. M5B 1M4
Tel: (416) 363-3171
Federal Publications Inc.,
301-303 King St. W.,
Toronto, Ont. M5V 1J5
Tel. (416)581-1552
Les Éditions la Liberté inc.,
3020 Chemin Sainte-Foy,
Sainte-Foy, P.Q. GIX 3V6,
Tel. (418)658-3763

**DENMARK - DANEMARK**
Munksgaard Export and Subscription Service
35, Nørre Søgade, DK-1370 København K
Tel. +45.1.12.85.70

**FINLAND - FINLANDE**
Akateeminen Kirjakauppa,
Keskuskatu 1, 00100 Helsinki 10   Tel. 0.12141

**FRANCE**
OCDE/OECD
Mail Orders/Commandes par correspondance :
2, rue André-Pascal,
75775 Paris Cedex 16
Tel. (1) 45.24.82.00
Bookshop/Librairie : 33, rue Octave-Feuillet
75016 Paris
Tel. (1) 45.24.81.67 or/ou (1) 45.24.81.81
Librairie de l'Université,
12a, rue Nazareth,
13602 Aix-en-Provence       Tel. 42.26.18.08

**GERMANY - ALLEMAGNE**
OECD Publications and Information Centre,
4 Simrockstrasse,
5300 Bonn        Tel. (0228) 21.60.45

**GREECE - GRÈCE**
Librairie Kauffmann,
28, rue du Stade, 105 64 Athens  Tel. 322.21.60

**HONG KONG**
Government Information Services,
Publications (Sales) Office,
Information Services Department
No. 1, Battery Path, Central

**ICELAND - ISLANDE**
Snæbjörn Jónsson & Co., h.f.,
Hafnarstræti 4 & 9,
P.O.B. 1131 – Reykjavik
Tel. 13133/14281/11936

**INDIA - INDE**
Oxford Book and Stationery Co.,
Scindia House, New Delhi 110001
Tel. 331.5896/5308
17 Park St., Calcutta 700016      Tel. 240832

**INDONESIA - INDONÉSIE**
Pdii-Lipi, P.O. Box 3065/JKT.Jakarta
Tel. 583467

**IRELAND - IRLANDE**
TDC Publishers - Library Suppliers,
12 North Frederick Street, Dublin 1
Tel. 744835-749677

**ITALY - ITALIE**
Libreria Commissionaria Sansoni,
Via Lamarmora 45, 50121 Firenze
Tel. 579751/584468
Via Bartolini 29, 20155 Milano    Tel. 365083
La diffusione delle pubblicazioni OCSE viene
assicurata dalle principali librerie ed anche da :
Editrice e Libreria Herder,
Piazza Montecitorio 120, 00186 Roma
Tel. 6794628
Libreria Hœpli,
Via Hœpli 5, 20121 Milano      Tel. 865446
Libreria Scientifica
Dott. Lucio de Biasio "Aeiou"
Via Meravigli 16, 20123 Milano   Tel. 807679

**JAPAN - JAPON**
OECD Publications and Information Centre,
Landic Akasaka Bldg., 2-3-4 Akasaka,
Minato-ku, Tokyo 107        Tel. 586.2016

**KOREA - CORÉE**
Kyobo Book Centre Co. Ltd.
P.O.Box: Kwang Hwa Moon 1658,
Seoul        Tel. (REP) 730.78.91

**LEBANON - LIBAN**
Documenta Scientifica/Redico,
Edison Building, Bliss St.,
P.O.B. 5641, Beirut      Tel. 354429-344425

**MALAYSIA/SINGAPORE -
MALAISIE/SINGAPOUR**
University of Malaya Co-operative Bookshop
Ltd.,
7 Lrg 51A/227A, Petaling Jaya
Malaysia        Tel. 7565000/7565425
Information Publications Pte Ltd
Pei-Fu Industrial Building,
24 New Industrial Road No. 02-06
Singapore 1953      Tel. 2831786, 2831798

**NETHERLANDS - PAYS-BAS**
SDU Uitgeverij
Christoffel Plantijnstraat 2
Postbus 20014
2500 EA's-Gravenhage      Tel. 070-789911
Voor bestellingen:        Tel. 070-789880

**NEW ZEALAND - NOUVELLE-ZÉLANDE**
Government Printing Office Bookshops:
Auckland: Retail Bookshop, 25 Rutland Stseet,
Mail Orders, 85 Beach Road
Private Bag C.P.O.
Hamilton: Retail: Ward Street,
Mail Orders, P.O. Box 857
Wellington: Retail, Mulgrave Street, (Head
Office)
Cubacade World Trade Centre,
Mail Orders, Private Bag
Christchurch: Retail, 159 Hereford Street,
Mail Orders, Private Bag
Dunedin: Retail, Princes Street,
Mail Orders, P.O. Box 1104

**NORWAY - NORVÈGE**
Narvesen Info Center – NIC,
Bertrand Narvesens vei 2,
P.O.B. 6125 Etterstad, 0602 Oslo 6
Tel. (02) 67.83.10, (02) 68.40.20

**PAKISTAN**
Mirza Book Agency
65 Shahrah Quaid-E-Azam, Lahore 3 Tel. 66839

**PHILIPPINES**
I.J. Sagun Enterprises, Inc.
P.O. Box 4322 CPO Manila
Tel. 695-1946, 922-9495

**PORTUGAL**
Livraria Portugal,
Rua do Carmo 70-74,
1117 Lisboa Codex        Tel. 360582/3

**SINGAPORE/MALAYSIA -
SINGAPOUR/MALAISIE**
See "Malaysia/Singapor". Voir
«Malaisie/Singapour»

**SPAIN - ESPAGNE**
Mundi-Prensa Libros, S.A.,
Castelló 37, Apartado 1223, Madrid-28001
Tel. 431.33.99
Libreria Bosch, Ronda Universidad 11,
Barcelona 7      Tel. 317.53.08/317.53.58

**SWEDEN - SUÈDE**
AB CE Fritzes Kungl. Hovbokhandel,
Box 16356, S 103 27 STH,
Regeringsgatan 12,
DS Stockholm        Tel. (08) 23.89.00
Subscription Agency/Abonnements:
Wennergren-Williams AB,
Box 30004, S104 25 Stockholm Tel. (08)54.12.00

**SWITZERLAND - SUISSE**
OECD Publications and Information Centre,
4 Simrockstrasse,
5300 Bonn (Germany)     Tel. (0228) 21.60.45
Librairie Payot,
6 rue Grenus, 1211 Genève 11
Tel. (022) 31.89.50
United Nations Bookshop/Librairie des Nations-
Unies
Palais des Nations,
1211 – Geneva 10
Tel. 022-34-60-11 (ext. 48 72)

**TAIWAN - FORMOSE**
Good Faith Worldwide Int'l Co., Ltd.
9th floor, No. 118, Sec.2
Chung Hsiao E. Road
Taipei        Tel. 391.7396/391.7397

**THAILAND - THAILANDE**
Suksit Siam Co., Ltd., 1715 Rama IV Rd.,
Samyam Bangkok 5      Tel. 2511630
INDEX Book Promotion & Service Ltd.
59/6 Soi Lang Suan, Ploenchit Road
Patjumamwan, Bangkok 10500
Tel. 250-1919, 252-1066

**TURKEY - TURQUIE**
Kültur Yayinlari Is-Türk Ltd. Sti.
Atatürk Bulvari No: 191/Kat. 21
Kavaklidere/Ankara      Tel. 25.07.60
Dolmabahce Cad. No: 29
Besiktas/Istanbul      Tel. 160.71.88

**UNITED KINGDOM - ROYAUME-UNI**
H.M. Stationery Office,
Postal orders only:        (01)211-5656
P.O.B. 276, London SW8 5DT
Telephone orders: (01) 622.3316, or
Personal callers:
49 High Holborn, London WC1V 6HB
Branches at: Belfast, Birmingham,
Bristol, Edinburgh, Manchester

**UNITED STATES - ÉTATS-UNIS**
OECD Publications and Information Centre,
2001 L Street, N.W., Suite 700,
Washington, D.C. 20036 - 4095
Tel. (202) 785.6323

**VENEZUELA**
Libreria del Este,
Avda F. Miranda 52, Aptdo. 60337,
Edificio Galipan, Caracas 106
Tel. 951.17.05/951.23.07/951.12.97

**YUGOSLAVIA - YOUGOSLAVIE**
Jugoslovenska Knjiga, Knez Mihajlova 2,
P.O.B. 36, Beograd      Tel. 621.992

Orders and inquiries from countries where
Distributors have not yet been appointed should be
sent to:
OECD, Publications Service, 2, rue André-Pascal,
75775 PARIS CEDEX 16.

Les commandes provenant de pays où l'OCDE n'a
pas encore désigné de distributeur doivent être
adressées à :
OCDE, Service des Publications. 2, rue André-
Pascal, 75775 PARIS CEDEX 16.

71784-07-1988

OECD PUBLICATIONS, 2, rue André-Pascal, 75775 PARIS CEDEX 16 - No. 44567 1988
PRINTED IN FRANCE
(97 88 08 1) ISBN 92-64-13156-6

8

9909